HOW IT WORKS

AF082906

SPACE

STUART CLARK

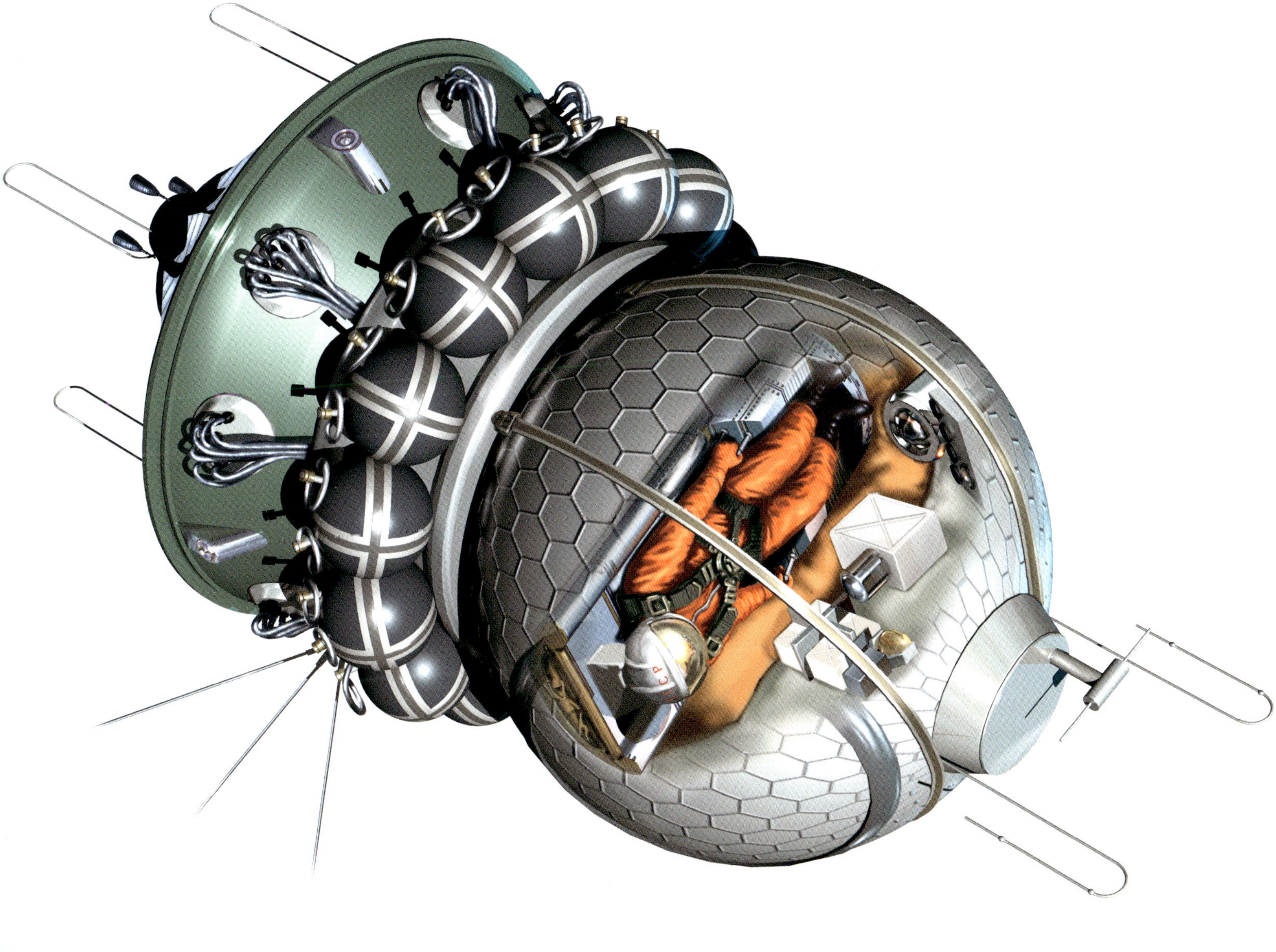

award

Series editor: Elizabeth Miles
Cover design: Duck Egg Blue
Illustrations and photographs: Jeff Bowles, David Hardy, Sebastian Quigley, Mike Saunders, Steve Weston, Gerald Witcomb, NASA, NASA Images, NASA/CXC/M.Weiss, NASA/ESA/CSA/STScI, NASA/ESA/Northrop Grumman, NASA/GSFC, NASA/Johns Hopkins University Applied Physics Laboratory/Southwest Research Institute/Alex Parker, NASA Johnson, NASA/JPL, NASA/JPL-Caltech, NASA/JPL-Caltech/GSFC/JAXA, NASA/JPL-Caltech/SSC, NASA/JPL/Malin Space Science Systems, NASA/JPL/University of Arizona, NASA/JPL/University of Arizona/University of Idaho, NASA/JPL/DLR, NASA/Johns Hopkins University Applied Physics Laboratory/Carnegie Institution of Washington, NASA/Space Telescope Science Institute, Shutterstock.com (Alex Mit, Dotted Yeti, Kristian D. Hansen, Magdanatka, NASA Images, Nerthuz, Radek Karko, Rashevska Nataliia, sumikophoto, Vadim Sadovski)

ISBN 978-1-78270-006-7

Copyright © Award Publications Limited

All rights reserved. No part of this publication may be reproduced or utilised in any form or by any means electronic or mechanical, including photocopying, recording, or by any information storage and retrieval system now known or hereafter invented, without the prior written permission of the publisher.

This edition first published 2025

Published by Award Publications Limited,
The Old Riding School, Welbeck,
Worksop, S80 3LR

/awardpublications @award.books
www.awardpublications.co.uk

23-1100 1

Printed in China

Contents

The Big Bang	6
The Universe	8
The Solar System	10
The Planets	12
Planet Earth	14
Rocket Power	16
Early Missions	18
Project Apollo	20
On the Moon	22
Space Shuttle	24
Space Walking	26
Space Stations	28
Viking Lander	30
Mars Pathfinder	32
Voyager	34
Studying the Stars	36
Stars	38
Black Holes	40
Radio Telescopes	42
Magnetic Fields	44
Index	46

The Big Bang

Astronomers believe that the Universe began about 13.7 billion years ago with an event known as the Big Bang. At the time of the Big Bang, the Universe began as the smallest of points and then suddenly began to expand. In about the same amount of time as it would take you to read this page, all the matter (material) that became everything we see today in the Universe was created. Even the particles that make up this book were formed in the first few seconds after the Big Bang.

At first, everything was crammed into a tiny space, so the Universe was very dense. At this point, atoms, the building blocks of matter, began to form. As time went by and the Universe expanded more, it became less dense. Today, space is mostly empty, with dense parts (the planets, stars and galaxies) only dotted around here and there.

Quark Electron Proton Neutron

Formation of matter

A millionth of a second after the Big Bang, simple particles called quarks and electrons appeared. Quarks then joined together to form neutrons and protons. A single proton is known as a hydrogen nucleus. Later, neutrons and protons joined together to make helium nuclei. Finally, electrons began to orbit these nuclei and turn them into atoms.

The first stars formed, but planets like the Earth could not yet form around them

Galaxies become elliptical if they collide with another large galaxy

After 300,000 years, the temperature had cooled enough for atoms to form

The first seconds

In the beginning, the Universe was a frenzy of activity. Matter existed only in the form of electrons and simple particles called quarks. These quarks were not yet stable and kept turning into energy. The energy then turned back into quarks.

Space suddenly inflated (expanded) to many times the size it had been and quarks became stable

The temperature dropped and the quarks formed neutrons and protons

After a few minutes, a quarter of all matter had been turned into helium

After one billion years, galaxies began to form – they started as huge, collapsing clouds of gas

Hydrogen nucleus Helium nucleus Hydrogen atom Helium atom

Planets like the Earth formed around stars

Our Solar System is located in the Milky Way galaxy

The Universe is now about 13.7 billion years old and continues to expand

Ten billion years after the Big Bang, the Sun and the planets in our Solar System formed

Birth of a solar system

Solar systems such as ours formed when gas clouds in galaxies collapsed. First, a gas cloud began to shrink and a star began to form at its centre (1). As the cloud collapsed further, gases gathered in a disc around the star (2). The gases in this disc collided and stuck together, gradually turning into dust grains. The dust grains continued to become larger in this way until, after tens of thousands of years, planets were formed and a solar system was born (3).

The Universe

The Universe is so large that astronomers measure most distances in light years. One light year is 9.5 trillion kilometres – the distance that light travels in a year. A ray of light travels at 300,000 kilometres a second, which is faster than anything else in the Universe.

There are many different types of object found in the Universe. Some are very large and others are tiny. The largest are gigantic filaments, which are made up of superclusters. These contain clusters (groups) of galaxies. Galaxies are the homes of stars. A spiral galaxy, such as our Milky Way galaxy, is about 100,000 light years across. Some galaxies are still forming new stars today, but others stopped making stars millions of years ago. Planets can be found orbiting (moving in a circle around) some stars. The smallest solid objects in the Universe are the tiny particles of dust that lie between the planets.

Types of galaxies

Galaxies can be split into three types: elliptical galaxies (1); spiral galaxies, like Andromeda, with curved arms of stars (2); and barred-spiral galaxies which have a bar of stars between their arms and their centres (3).

The nearest spiral galaxy to ours is called Andromeda

The observable Universe is a sphere with a diameter of 93 billion light years

Gigantic filaments are made up of superclusters

There are many large, empty voids in the Universe today

Superclusters of galaxies can be hundreds of millions of light years long. They contain many clusters of galaxies

Individual clusters can contain several thousand galaxies

The Milky Way is part of a small cluster of galaxies known as the Local Group. The Milky Way is surrounded by smaller satellite galaxies

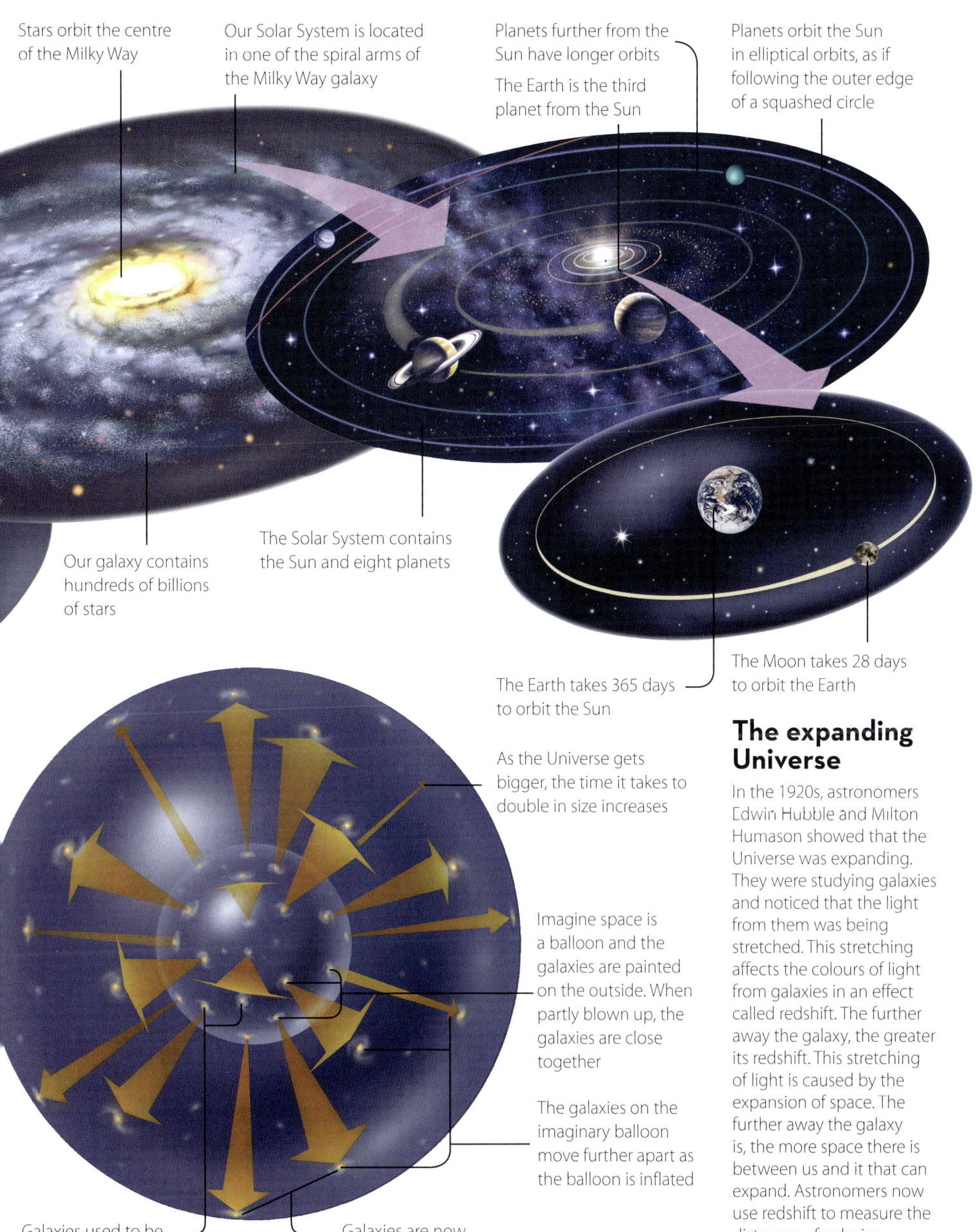

Stars orbit the centre of the Milky Way

Our Solar System is located in one of the spiral arms of the Milky Way galaxy

Planets further from the Sun have longer orbits

The Earth is the third planet from the Sun

Planets orbit the Sun in elliptical orbits, as if following the outer edge of a squashed circle

Our galaxy contains hundreds of billions of stars

The Solar System contains the Sun and eight planets

The Moon takes 28 days to orbit the Earth

The Earth takes 365 days to orbit the Sun

As the Universe gets bigger, the time it takes to double in size increases

Imagine space is a balloon and the galaxies are painted on the outside. When partly blown up, the galaxies are close together

The galaxies on the imaginary balloon move further apart as the balloon is inflated

Galaxies used to be closer together

Galaxies are now further apart

The expanding Universe

In the 1920s, astronomers Edwin Hubble and Milton Humason showed that the Universe was expanding. They were studying galaxies and noticed that the light from them was being stretched. This stretching affects the colours of light from galaxies in an effect called redshift. The further away the galaxy, the greater its redshift. This stretching of light is caused by the expansion of space. The further away the galaxy is, the more space there is between us and it that can expand. Astronomers now use redshift to measure the distances of galaxies.

The Solar System

We live on Earth. The Earth belongs to a family of eight planets that orbit the Sun. Both the planets and the Sun formed about 4.6 billion years ago and together they are known as the Solar System. The four inner planets – Mercury, Venus, Earth and Mars – are all similar. They are rocky worlds, but only Earth has an atmosphere (the gas surrounding a planet) that humans can breathe.

Beyond Mars is the asteroid belt. This band contains millions and millions of rocks that also orbit the Sun. Still further away are four larger planets: Jupiter, Saturn, Uranus and Neptune. These 'gas giants' have very thick atmospheres and no solid surfaces. Jupiter is the largest planet. Beyond the gas giants is Pluto, which was once called a planet but is now classed as a 'dwarf planet', along with other small, icy worlds that orbit in the outer part of the Solar System.

Orbits

The planets are held in the Solar System by the pull of the Sun's gravity. The Sun contains so much matter that its force of gravity is very large and causes the planets to move in orbits around it. The patterns of these orbits are similar to circles.

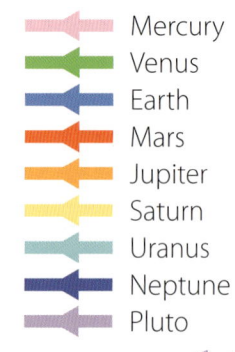

- Mercury
- Venus
- Earth
- Mars
- Jupiter
- Saturn
- Uranus
- Neptune
- Pluto

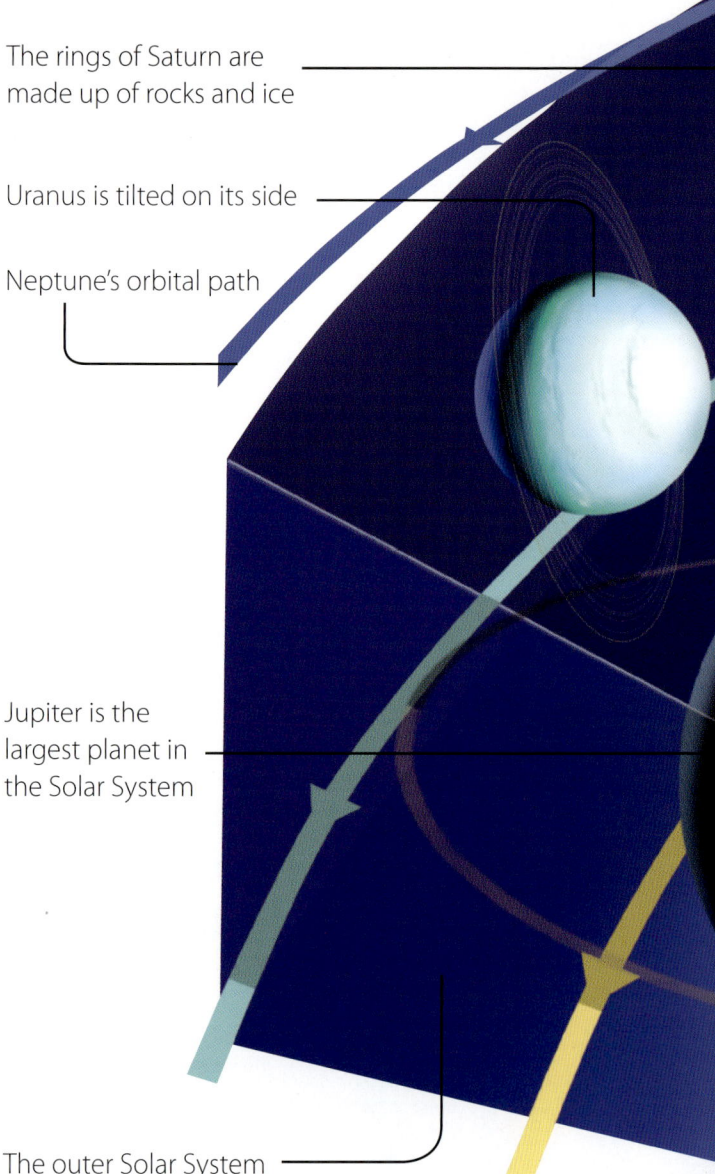

Pluto, a dwarf planet, is covered in ice

The rings of Saturn are made up of rocks and ice

Uranus is tilted on its side

Neptune's orbital path

Jupiter is the largest planet in the Solar System

The outer Solar System

Asteroids were discovered by astronomers looking for a planet between Mars and Jupiter

The Galaxy

The Sun is one of billions of stars which make up our galaxy. Also known as the Milky Way, the galaxy has a flat, spiral shape. The Sun is not at the centre. In fact, it is in one of the spiral arms, closer to the galaxy's edge than its centre. Its position is shown by the red dots below. The Sun orbits the centre of the galaxy once every 220,000,000 years. Our galaxy is one of billions of galaxies in the Universe.

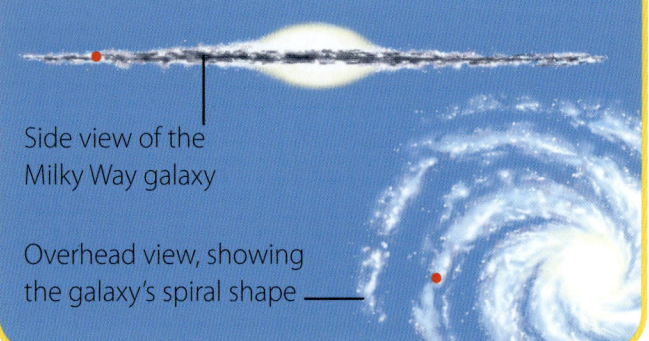

Side view of the Milky Way galaxy

Overhead view, showing the galaxy's spiral shape

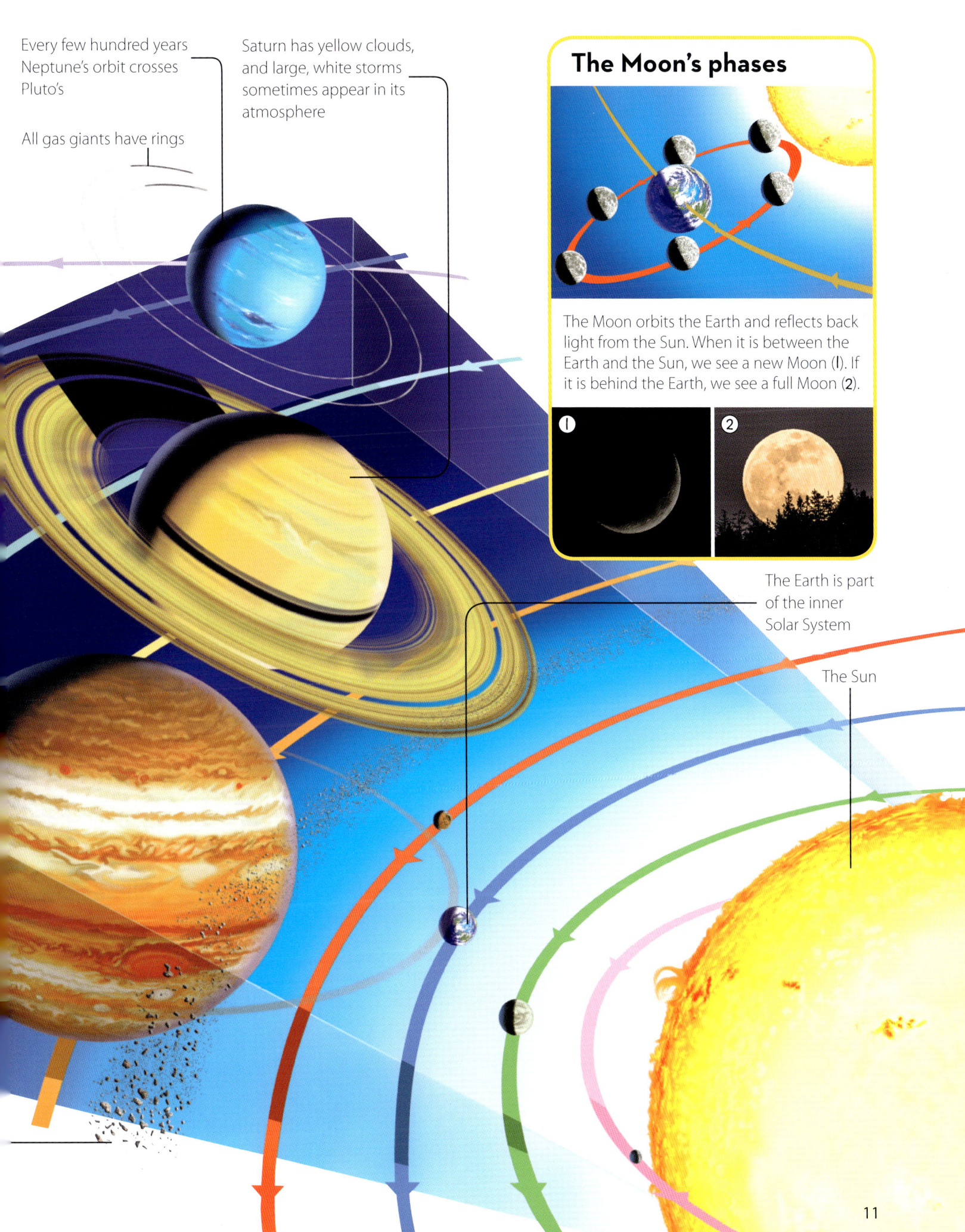

Every few hundred years Neptune's orbit crosses Pluto's

Saturn has yellow clouds, and large, white storms sometimes appear in its atmosphere

All gas giants have rings

The Moon's phases

The Moon orbits the Earth and reflects back light from the Sun. When it is between the Earth and the Sun, we see a new Moon (1). If it is behind the Earth, we see a full Moon (2).

The Earth is part of the inner Solar System

The Sun

The Planets

All eight planets of the Solar System orbit the Sun but each one is unique. Many have moons in orbit around them. The four 'gas giants' – Uranus, Jupiter, Neptune and Saturn – have rings as well.

The matter inside a planet or moon is found in layers. The densest material is at the centre and is usually made up of iron. The outer material consists of rock. Gas, which is a planet's lightest material, sits above the planet's surface and is called the atmosphere. This layering of the planets and moons shows that when they formed, they were made of molten lava. Collisions with other new planets had made their rock melt. While it was molten, heavier materials sank to the centre and lighter materials rose to the surface.

Moons

Earth's Moon is rocky with a small iron core (1). There are many other natural satellites, mostly around the gas giants. Jupiter's moons include Europa (2), which scientists think has an ocean beneath its icy crust, and Io (3), which has the most volcanoes in the Solar System. Saturn's largest moon, Titan (4), is always covered in cloud.

Jupiter's Great Red Spot is a storm as large as planet Earth

Pluto's moon, Charon, was discovered in 1978

Pluto

Pluto (*above*) is a dwarf planet. It is much smaller than Earth and is made up of ice surrounding a core of rock and iron. It is orbited by five natural satellites, the largest of which is Charon.

Uranus

This blue-green gas giant (*below, right*) has a thick atmosphere of gas over an even thicker icy layer of water, methane and ammonia. It has a small rocky core about the size of the Earth at its centre.

Narrow rings around Uranus are made up of small, dark dust particles

Jupiter

Jupiter's diameter is eleven times that of Earth. Below its surface is a mixture of hydrogen and helium gas that is under so much pressure from the atmosphere that it behaves like a liquid. Below this, the mixture is compressed even more and acts like a liquid metal. In the very centre of the planet there may be a rock and iron core five times bigger than Earth.

Neptune

The planet Neptune (*left*) is about the same size as Uranus. It also has a similar inner structure. The rings of Neptune are patchy. Some areas are rather dense whilst others are sparse.

Mercury

Mercury (*left*) is the closest planet to the Sun. It has a large iron core covered by a layer of rocky material. On top is the crust, cratered by collisions with smaller objects such as asteroids.

Venus

Venus (*left*) is almost the same size as Earth but is otherwise very different. It is permanently covered in clouds of carbon dioxide and its surface is hotter than an oven.

The clouds around Venus hide a landscape of cliffs, valleys, highlands and lowlands

The Mariner Valley is about 4,000 kilometres long

Mars

The diameter of Mars (*above*) is about half that of Earth. It has a very large rift valley called the Mariner Valley, named after the space probe that discovered it.

Saturn is the flattest of the planets. Its squashed sphere shape is caused by its low density and fast rotation

Saturn's rings have gaps caused by the gravity of its moons

Saturn

The interior of Saturn is similar to that of Jupiter. One difference between them is that inside Saturn it is possible for helium gas to become a liquid. It then falls as rain into the central region of the planet.

Planet Earth

Earth is the planet on which we live. It formed with the Sun and other planets 4.6 billion years ago. Originally, Earth was a sphere of lava (molten rock). Heavy chemicals such as iron sank into the planet, while lighter ones floated to the top. Water and the atmospheric gases that allow us to live and breathe were brought to the planet by colliding balls of ice known as comets.

Earth has a core of iron surrounded by a large region of molten rock, called the mantle. Heat travelling through the outer mantle causes the molten rock to move in large oval pathways. The rocky crust of the Earth is broken into large pieces called plates. These float on the mantle. Where they collide, earthquakes occur and volcanoes erupt.

The Earth's core

The Earth's core contains one third of our planet's mass. Geologists have monitored the way in which sounds travel through the Earth and discovered that the core is divided into two regions. The outer core is made up of liquid iron. The inner core is solid iron.

Heat from inside the Earth makes the outer mantle's molten rock convect (move in circular patterns)

The thin crust is made up of pieces (plates) of solidified rock. Ocean plates form the ocean floor; continental plates form the land

Convection in the outer core causes Earth to generate a magnetic field

Where ocean plates collide, one is forced down into the mantle

Inner mantle rocks are pressed solid by the weight above

In the outer mantle, the rock is molten

When it is winter in the Northern Hemisphere, it is summer in the Southern Hemisphere

Mountain ranges are created by colliding plates

Clouds are formed by water vapour in the Earth's atmosphere

The South Pole is opposite the North Pole

Earth's rotation about its axis gives us night and day

The seasons

As it orbits the Sun, the spinning Earth is always tilted at the same angle. When the north pole is tilted towards the Sun, it is summer in the north (1). Six months later, it is tilted away and it is winter (2). In between are the seasons spring (3) and autumn (4).

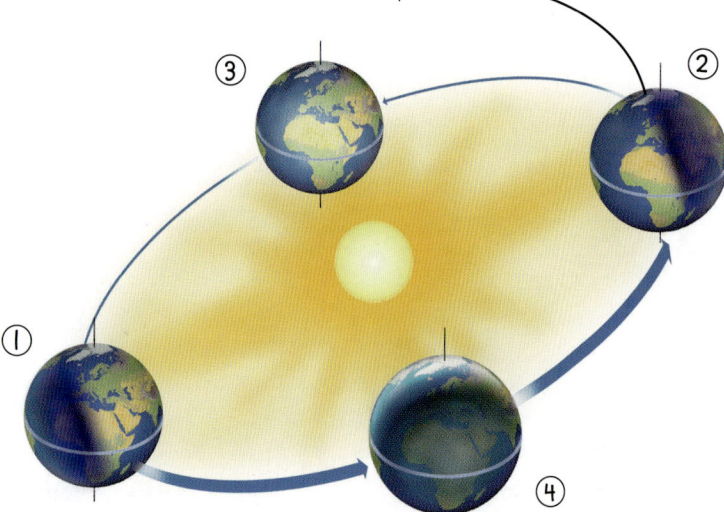

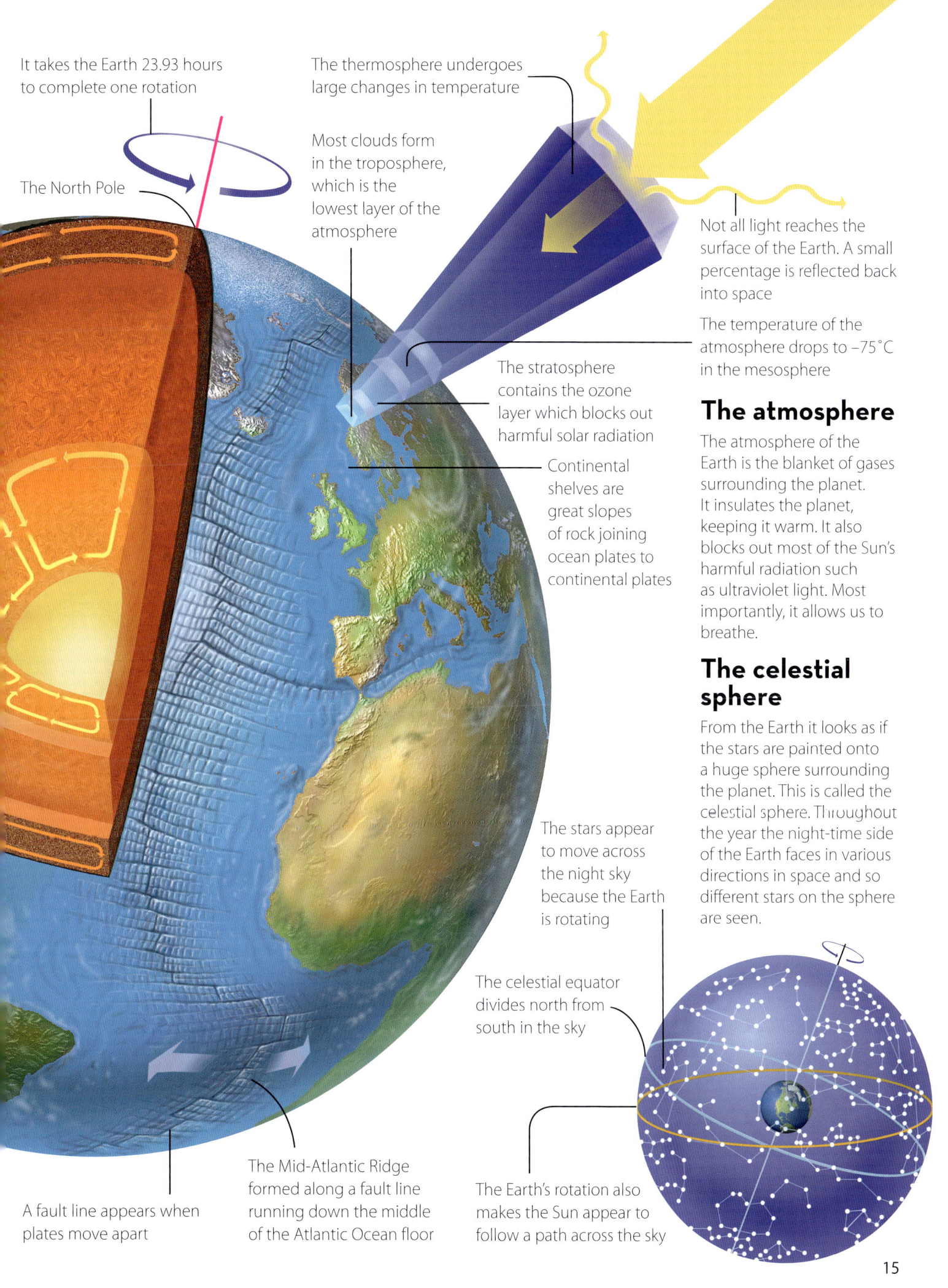

Rocket Power

The concept of the rocket can be traced as far back as Ancient Greece in the 4th century BC. In the 13th century AD, the Chinese built rockets using gunpowder and bamboo tubes that were launched attached to arrows. In peaceful times, rockets were used as fireworks, but during wars they were weapons.

The principle behind how a rocket works is that every action creates an equal and opposite reaction. This was stated as a law of nature by Sir Isaac Newton in 1687. If an explosion produces gas and that gas can be directed out of a tube, the gas leaving the tube will cause the tube itself to move in the opposite direction.

Rockets blast off from launch pads and take objects, such as communications satellites or a crew, into space. Some modern rockets, such as the Falcon 9 and Falcon Heavy, can return to Earth and land so they can be reused.

Until the launch of NASA's Space Launch System (SLS) in 2022, the most powerful rocket ever flown was the Saturn V, which launched astronauts to the Moon; it was over 110 metres high.

Satellites that are carried into orbit are known as the payload

This satellite is a telescope to be placed in a low Earth orbit

Payloads must be designed to fit into the rocket from which they will be launched

Stages

Although early rockets consisted of single engines, scientists soon realised that rockets should be built in stages. A stage is a section of the rocket that falls away when its fuel is used up. This reduces the rocket's mass so that it can be accelerated more easily by the next stage's engines.

The Saturn V and Soyuz are three-stage rockets. The large first stage lifts the rocket from the ground. When its fuel tanks are empty, it is cast off and the second stage's engines take over. Finally, a third stage places the rocket and its payload into orbit.

Satellites may have small rockets of their own to place them in their final orbits

Ariane 4 was a European-built rocket, launched from South America. It was 60 metres high

History of rockets

Early in the 20th century, an American called Robert Goddard launched the first modern rocket (**1**). It flew to a height of 12.5 metres. Rockets have always been used as weapons and in the Second World War, Germany developed the V-2 rocket (**2**) to launch attacks on London. Many countries have developed rockets. Russia built the R-7 family of rockets to launch their Vostok and Soyuz missions (**3**). The Saturn V rocket (**4**) was developed by America for the Apollo Moon missions, and the Space Shuttle (**5**) was the first reusable spacecraft.

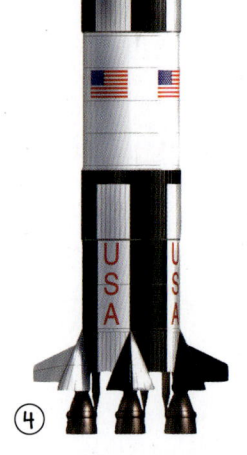

- Once in space, the fairing (casing around the payload) splits in two and the satellites are released
- This satellite is a communications satellite to be placed in a high orbit
- Large payload bay

Flight path

The Ariane rocket took off (1) using the first stage and the strap-on boosters. When the boosters were out of fuel they were cast off (2). Shortly afterwards, the first stage also ran out of fuel and was dropped (3). The fairing split (4) in preparation for releasing the satellites. The second stage used its fuel and was discarded (5). The first satellite was deployed (6) into a low Earth orbit (7). The second satellite was boosted to a much higher orbit (8).

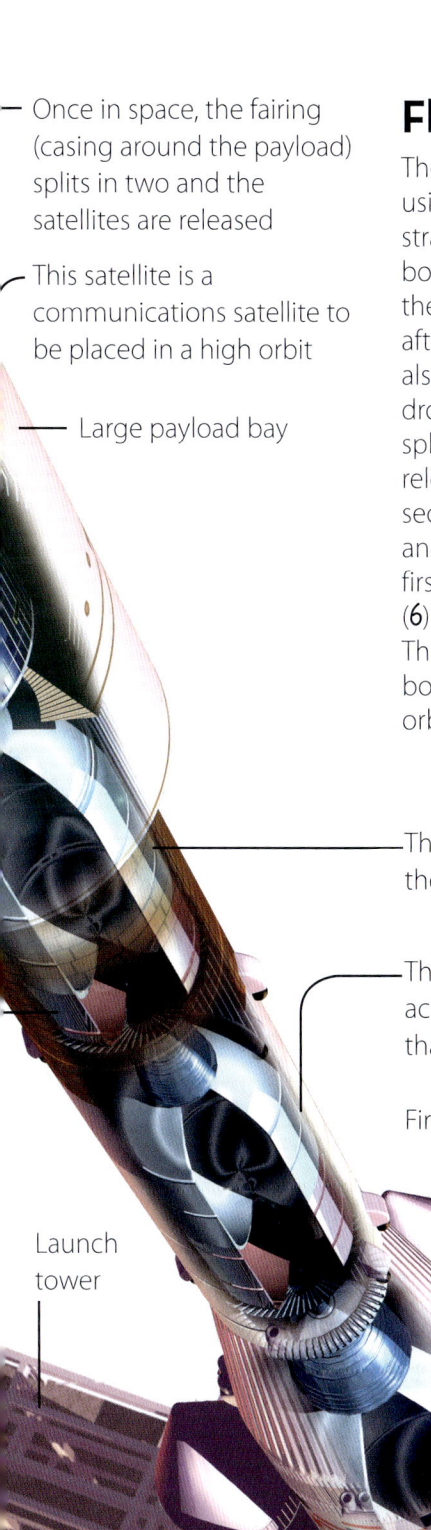

- The third-stage rocket lifts the satellites into orbit
- The second stage accelerates the rocket so that it travels twice as fast
- First-stage fuel tank
- Launch tower
- The first stage is helped by strap-on booster rockets
- First-stage oxygen tank
- First-stage rocket engines

- To achieve lift off, a rocket must produce enough thrust to overcome Earth's gravity
- Liquid hydrogen fuel is supplied to the rocket from the fuel tank
- Liquid oxygen is fed into a chamber where it mixes with the liquid hydrogen
- The combustion chamber lights the fuel and directs the thrust behind the rocket – this makes the rocket move upwards

Rocket fuel

Rocket engines ignite fuel to produce thrust. Liquid oxygen mixed with another liquid fuel, such as hydrogen or fluorine, produces more thrust than a single fuel could. In the future, rockets may use three fuels and gain even more energy.

Early Missions

The Soviet Union (now Russia) was the first country to place a human being in space. The cosmonaut Yuri Gagarin flew in the spacecraft Vostok 1 on 12 April 1961. His flight lasted just 89 minutes, but during that time he made a complete orbit of the Earth and then returned safely. Vostok 1 had been launched from what is now Kazakhstan by a rocket designed as a missile to carry explosives. The Russians launched Vostok 2 just a few months later on 6 August 1961. This time the cosmonaut stayed in space for a whole day.

A year later they launched cosmonauts in Vostok 3 and 4 with just 24 hours between the launches. Both spacecraft successfully returned to Earth a few days later. In 1963 Vostok 5 and 6 were launched. Vostok 6 carried Valentina Tereshkova, the first woman in space.

The instrument module

The instrument module was controlled by the scientists on the ground. It was equipped with rocket engines that could control the spacecraft's movement once it was in orbit. Communication antennae were also attached to it. The module was ejected and allowed to burn up as it re-entered the atmosphere.

Flight profile

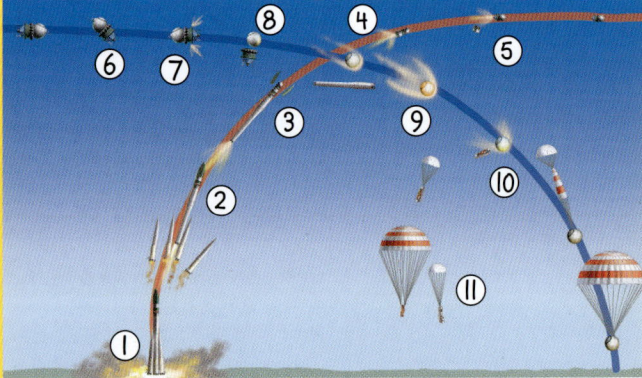

Vostok 1 blasts off (1) and drops the first-stage boosters (2). The nose casing is ejected as the second stage increases Vostok's speed (3). The final stage puts it in orbit (4) and then separates (5). After an orbit Vostok turns (6) and fires its retro-rocket (7). The instrument module is discarded (8) and Vostok 1 re-enters the atmosphere (9). The cosmonaut is ejected (10). Parachutes return the module and astronaut safely to Earth (11).

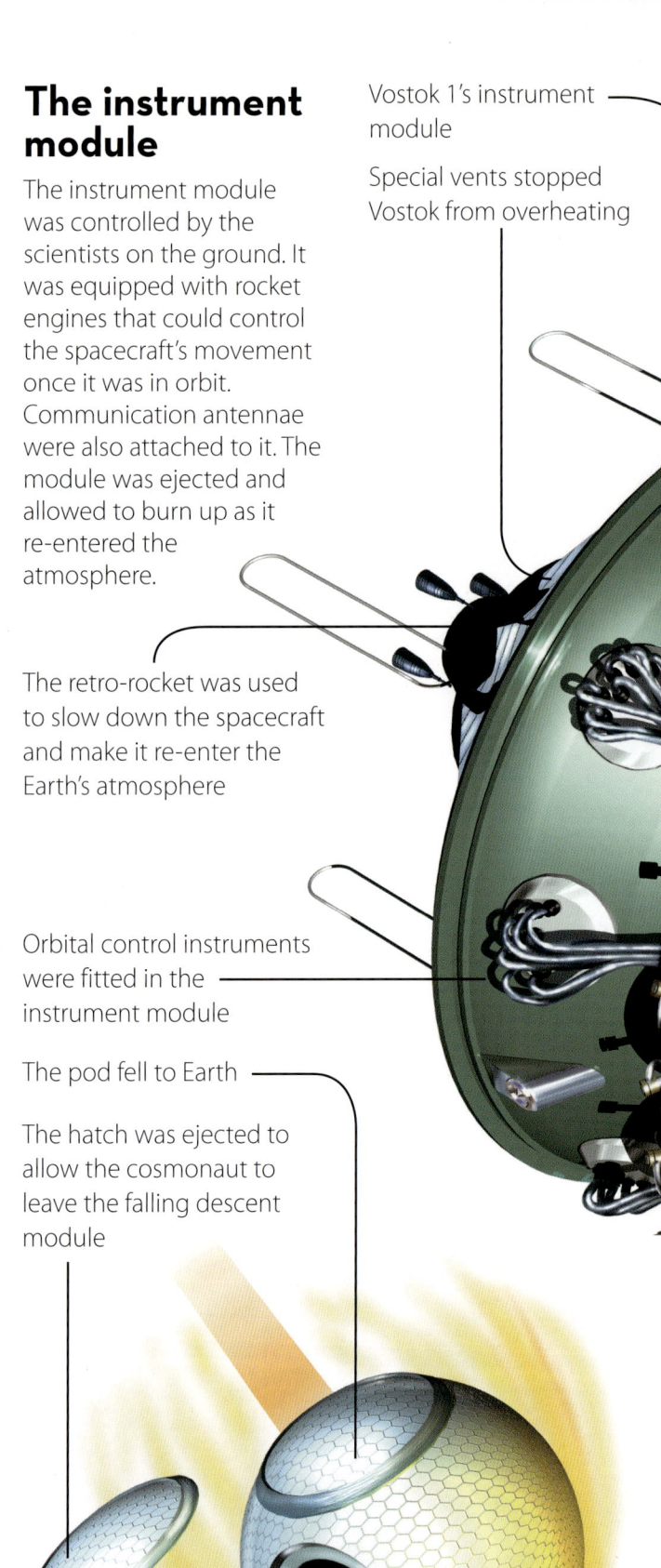

Vostok 1's instrument module

Special vents stopped Vostok from overheating

The retro-rocket was used to slow down the spacecraft and make it re-enter the Earth's atmosphere

Orbital control instruments were fitted in the instrument module

The pod fell to Earth

The hatch was ejected to allow the cosmonaut to leave the falling descent module

The cosmonaut was ejected from the capsule for landing

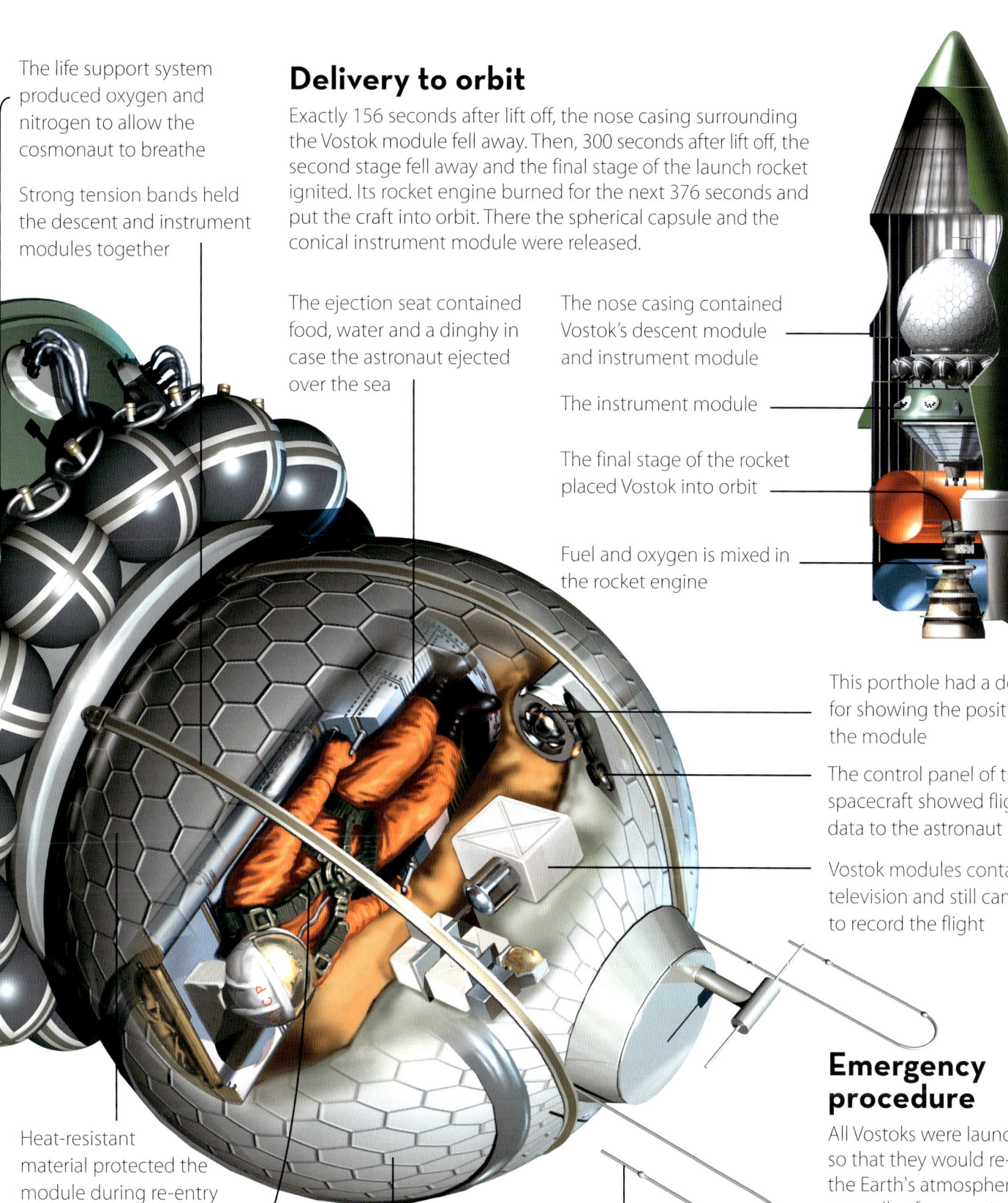

The life support system produced oxygen and nitrogen to allow the cosmonaut to breathe

Strong tension bands held the descent and instrument modules together

Delivery to orbit

Exactly 156 seconds after lift off, the nose casing surrounding the Vostok module fell away. Then, 300 seconds after lift off, the second stage fell away and the final stage of the launch rocket ignited. Its rocket engine burned for the next 376 seconds and put the craft into orbit. There the spherical capsule and the conical instrument module were released.

The ejection seat contained food, water and a dinghy in case the astronaut ejected over the sea

The nose casing contained Vostok's descent module and instrument module

The instrument module

The final stage of the rocket placed Vostok into orbit

Fuel and oxygen is mixed in the rocket engine

This porthole had a device for showing the position of the module

The control panel of the spacecraft showed flight data to the astronaut

Vostok modules contained television and still cameras to record the flight

Heat-resistant material protected the module during re-entry

Only in an emergency was the cosmonaut allowed to touch the spacecraft controls

The re-entry capsule measured 2.5 metres across

Communications antennae are fitted at the front and rear

Emergency procedure

All Vostoks were launched so that they would re-enter the Earth's atmosphere naturally after a period of ten days. This prevented the loss of the cosmonaut's life should the retro-rocket fail to slow the spacecraft down. In order to survive for ten days, the Vostok capsule was stocked with enough food and water, but this precaution was never needed.

Parachute landing

The Vostok modules landed on solid ground. Although the module was slowed by parachutes, the impact might have hurt the cosmonaut inside. So they were ejected at an altitude from which they could safely land using a separate parachute.

Project Apollo

One of the greatest achievements of the human race has been the space missions of the late 1960s and early 1970s, which placed humans on the Moon. On 20 July 1969, Apollo 11 touched down on the surface of the Moon. Shortly afterwards, astronaut Neil Armstrong became the first human being to walk on a world in the Solar System other than Earth.

Over three years, seven manned missions were launched to land on the Moon. Each carried three astronauts. One stayed in the command module and orbited around the Moon while the other two descended to the surface in the lunar module.

Apollo 13 almost became a disaster when an electrical system short-circuited and caused an explosion, destroying an oxygen tank. The landing on the Moon was abandoned and the astronauts returned safely to Earth. They used oxygen from the lunar module to keep themselves alive.

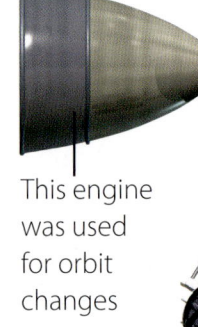

This engine was used for orbit changes

Command and service module

The command and service module was the astronauts' home during the voyages to and from the Moon. The conical section at the front is the command module, where the astronauts sat. It separated from the service module and re-entered the Earth's atmosphere when the mission was complete.

This radar dish helped the modules to reconnect

A hatch for getting into and out of the landing module

The ascent-stage rocket engine

Oxidiser from this tank mixes with rocket fuel to fire the main descent engine

A ladder for the crew to climb down onto the Moon

Landing legs absorb the shock of landing

When landing, as soon as one of these three sensing probes touched the Moon's surface, the engines were turned off

Arriving at the Moon

When the Apollo spacecraft arrived at the Moon it was made up of the command and service module (CSM) and lunar module joined together. With the CSM facing backwards, its engine was fired to put the spacecraft into lunar orbit. Two astronauts climbed into the lunar module. The lunar module then separated and fired its engine. This began the descent to the surface of the Moon to land.

The voyage between the Earth and Moon took about three days

The command and service module stayed in orbit

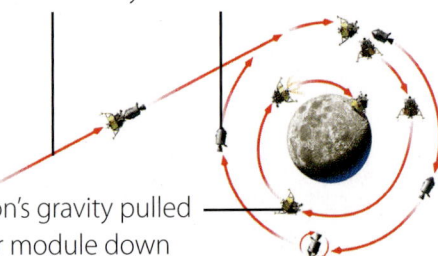

The Moon's gravity pulled the lunar module down

- Thrusters (small rockets) were used to change the direction the spacecraft faced
- The returning command module splashed down in the ocean
- Antennae allowed the modules to communicate
- A docking clamp grabbed on to the lunar module
- The docking hatch was at the top of the spacecraft
- Reaction control thrusters were used to keep the lunar module on course during landing and takeoff
- A fuel tank for the ascent from the Moon
- A fuel tank for the descent – more fuel was needed on descending than when returning to orbit
- The main descent engine slowed the lander as it went down
- The oxygen from this tank allowed the crew to breathe

Back to Earth

When the Moon walks were completed, the ascent stage of the lunar module lifted off and docked with the command and service module. The ascent stage was then undocked and allowded to fall back onto the Moon. The astronauts then travelled back to Earth. Firing its main engine put the command and service module on a course back to Earth

The lunar module

The lunar module (*left*) was the small spacecraft that carried the astronauts down to the surface of the Moon. It was made up of two parts, or stages. On top was the ascent stage. This contained the astronauts' cabin and the controls to fly the lunar module. Underneath was the descent stage, which had space to store equipment to be used on the Moon.

When it was time to leave the Moon, the descent stage was left behind. Because the Moon's gravitational pull is less powerful than it is on Earth, the ascent stage could take off with a smaller engine.

On the Moon

After Apollo 11 touched down on the Moon's surface, the astronauts prepared to go outside. During this first crewed Moon landing, the astronauts only made one trip outside the lunar module. Their moonwalk lasted two and a half hours. Then they climbed back aboard and prepared for take-off.

On each of the Apollo missions that followed, the astronauts spent longer and longer on the Moon. For Apollo 15, 16 and 17, each crew made several journeys away from the lander and spent over 18 hours exploring. Apollo 17, in December 1972, was the last manned mission to the Moon. Since then, ice has been discovered on the lunar surface. In the future, this could be used to provide drinking water and to produce rocket fuel, making longer stays possible.

Moon walking

While they were on the surface of the Moon, the astronauts performed many tasks. They collected rock samples and also left packages of experiments behind that continued to send information back to Earth long after the astronauts had left.

The rover's antenna was used to communicate with Mission Control

Still pictures were taken with this camera pack

The PLSS is strapped onto the spacesuit

The television camera filmed the lunar rover's journey

Electronics for the communication system

Portable life support system

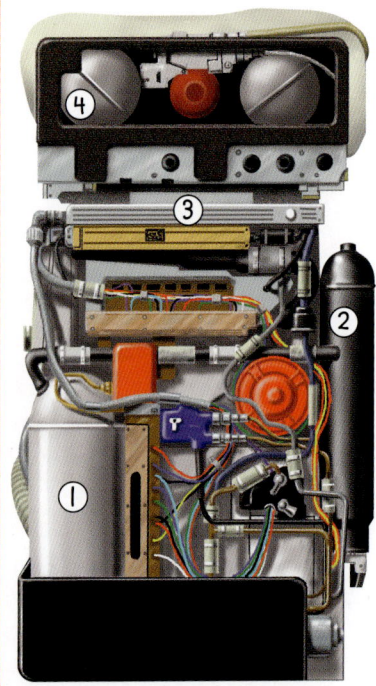

Because the Moon is so small, its gravity is not strong enough to hold air around it. This means that astronauts have to wear spacesuits to stay alive. The Apollo spacesuit was connected to a backpack called the Portable Life Support System (PLSS). The PLSS pumped oxygen (1) and water (2) to the spacesuit so that the astronaut could breathe and keep their body temperature normal. A radio (3) enabled the astronauts to talk to each other. An emergency oxygen supply (4) was also included.

Surveyor probes

Before humans set foot on the Moon, seven Surveyor landers were sent there. Cameras on the spacecraft took pictures of the surface, which helped scientists to choose Apollo landing sites.

Apollo 12 astronauts collected the TV camera from Surveyor 3

Rock samples were stored in the rover

The lunar module was the astronauts' home

Scoops were used to collect samples

382 kilograms of lunar rock were brought back to Earth from six Apollo missions

Controls for driving the rover

A display console helped astronauts to know the direction in which they were travelling

The rover's tyres were made of wire mesh

The rover was made of lightweight aluminium

Fenders stopped the rover and astronauts being covered with Moon dust

The lunar rover

Apollo 15, 16 and 17 each took a Lunar Roving Vehicle (LRV) to the Moon. It was folded up and stowed in one of the storage bays of the lunar module. On the Moon, it was unfolded from the side of the lunar module and used by the astronauts to explore further than they could on foot.

Space Shuttle

The Space Shuttle was the first spacecraft that could be used more than once. In the early days of space exploration, spacecraft were only able to fly a single mission. Most parts of the rocket burned up in the atmosphere or were left in space. The first Space Shuttle, called *Enterprise*, never flew in space but proved that such a large craft could glide successfully down to Earth.

The second Space Shuttle, *Columbia*, was launched in 1981. This was followed by *Challenger*, *Discovery*, *Atlantis* and *Endeavour*. In 1986, *Challenger* exploded shortly after lift-off, tragically killing all seven astronauts on board. In 2003, *Columbia* disintegrated during re-entry into the atmosphere at the end of its 28th mission. Again, the crew were lost.

The Shuttle worked in low Earth orbit (LEO) at an altitude of between 304 and 528 kilometres

The manoeuvring rockets were fired four times to place the Shuttle in orbit

Both scientific and communications satellites were launched by the Space Shuttle

The main fuel tank was jettisoned once it was empty

Booster rockets separated and fell into the ocean

The robot arm could grab or release satellites

The Space Shuttle was controlled by a pilot sitting on the flight deck

Shuttle flight profile

The Space Shuttle blasted off from Cape Canaveral in Florida, USA. At an altitude (height) of about 50 kilometres, the solid rocket boosters separated and fell back down to Earth. At an altitude of about 120 kilometres, the Shuttle ejected the main fuel tank, which was now empty. At this point the Shuttle was moving fast enough to reach orbit.

Small thrusters enabled the Shuttle to move within its orbit

At launch, the external fuel tank supported the body of the Shuttle

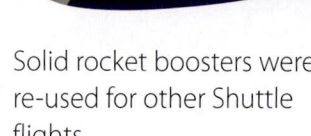

Solid rocket boosters were re-used for other Shuttle flights

The lower deck is where the astronauts lived and worked during the flight

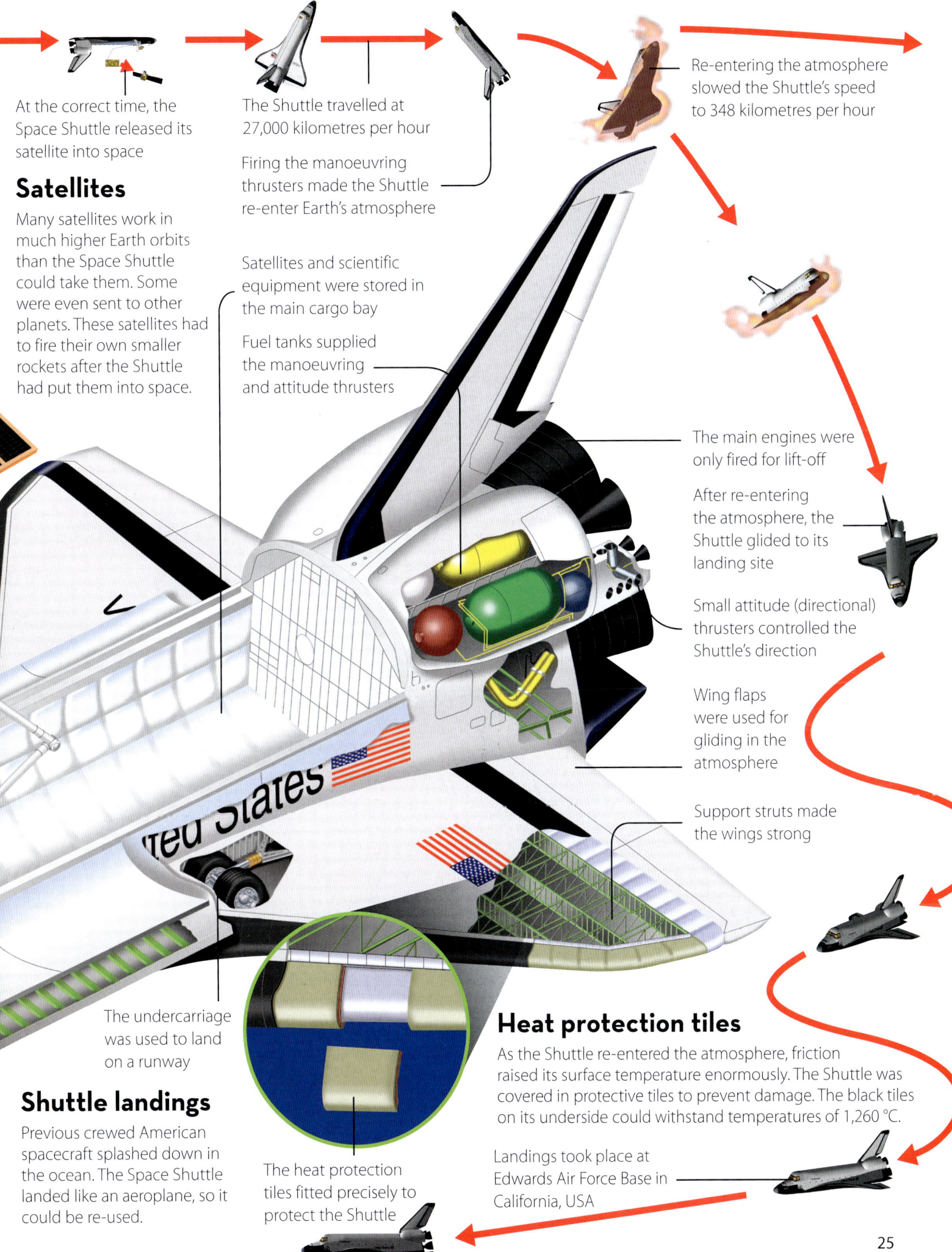

Spacewalking

There is no atmosphere for humans to breathe in space. Whenever work needs to be done outside a spacecraft, astronauts have to put on a spacesuit. Spacesuits keep the astronaut's body at the right temperature and supply them with oxygen to breathe and water to drink. On Earth, the pressure of the atmosphere prevents the fluids in our bodies from turning into gases. In space, a spacesuit must be pressurised to keep the astronaut's body fluids liquid.

On Earth and inside spacecraft, only one fifth of the gas breathed is oxygen, but in a spacesuit all of the gas is oxygen. Before astronauts can go outside, they must spend over two hours breathing nothing but oxygen through a mask in order to get used to it.

Video cameras recorded the spacewalks

Attitude jets

The attitude jets pushed the space walker along by blowing out nitrogen gas. The astronaut decided which way to move and pulled or twisted the control levers. A computer calculated which jet should be fired. For example, to make an astronaut turn, more than one jet was fired at the same time.

Nitrogen was stored in a tank and supplied to the attitude jets when needed

The backpack was known as the Manned Maneuvering Unit (MMU)

Electrical power to the MMU was supplied by a battery

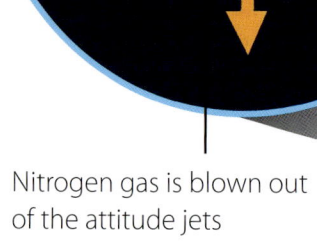

Nitrogen gas is blown out of the attitude jets

Attitude jets pointed out of the backpack in all directions

The Sun heated the spacesuit to over 100 °C

Working in space

When astronauts have to make repairs or install new equipment outside the International Space Station they might have to make a spacewalk. To be able to reach anywhere on the outside of the space station safely they can ride on a foot plate attached to the Canadarm2 Space Station Remote Manipulator System robotic arm (*left*).

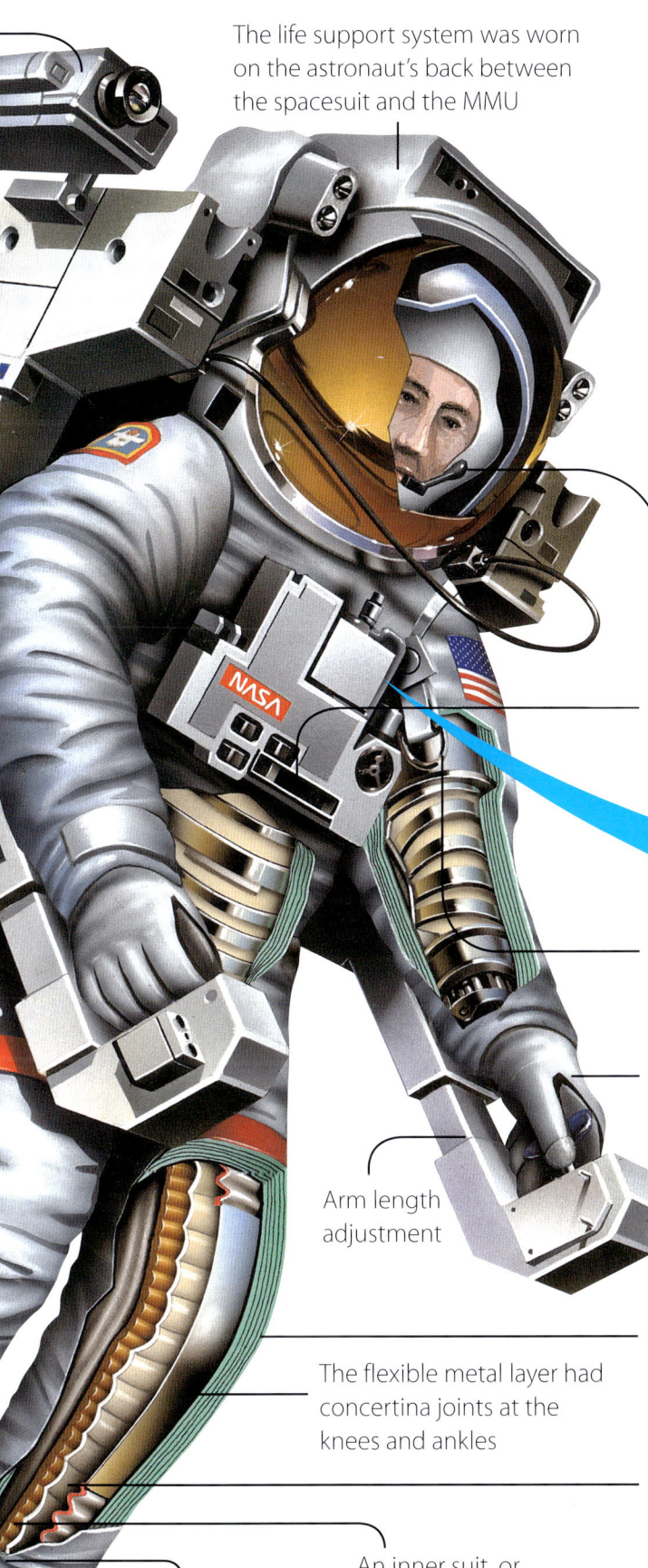

The life support system was worn on the astronaut's back between the spacesuit and the MMU

Lights enable astronauts to work when they are not in sunlight

The outer helmet protects the astronaut from the Sun's radiation

The cap contained headphones and a microphone for two-way communication

The upper part of the spacesuit was made of fibreglass to protect the astronaut from micrometeorites (dust particles in space)

Astronauts tethered themselves to the Shuttle for safety

Gloves had to fit well so astronauts could pick things up

Arm length adjustment

The outer layer of the spacesuit was fireproof

The flexible metal layer had concertina joints at the knees and ankles

The restraint layer prevented the pressure suit from inflating too much

The pressure suit filled with gas to simulate the weight of the Earth's atmosphere

An inner suit, or undergarment, contained water tubes that surrounded the astronaut's body to keep them at a comfortable temperature

Spacesuit control box

The controls to manage every aspect of the spacesuit were located on a box mounted on its front. If astronauts wanted to talk over the radio, they selected a channel (1), adjusted the volume (2), and pressed the switch (3) to talk. If they were too hot or cold, they could adjust the temperature of their spacesuit (4). More or less oxygen could be supplied by using a sliding control (5) and their water supply could be adjusted using a valve (6).

Space Stations

In 1971, the Soviet Union launched the first space station, Salyut 1. Early space stations only stayed in orbit for a few months, but as better systems were developed, they stayed in orbit for longer. The Russian space station, *Mir*, remained in orbit from 1986 to 2001.

The USA launched the Skylab space station (*below*) in 1973. Three crews of astronauts worked there for a total of 172 days. Almost six years later, in 1979, Skylab eventually burned up in the Earth's atmosphere. The International Space Station (*right*) is maintained by the USA, Russia, Canada, Japan and 11 countries of the European Space Agency. It continues to be modified as technology advances and mission requirements change.

Habitation module

The habitation module is one of the most important parts of the space station because it is where the astronauts live and sleep. Astronauts sleep near vents which take away the carbon dioxide they breathe out.

A strong lattice framework supports the space station

Solar panels are used to generate power

New modules can be fitted to the station at special connection points

A Russian Soyuz spacecraft remains permanently attached to the space station to serve as a 'lifeboat' in an emergency

An additional Soyuz spacecraft – used for transferring astronauts

Space station construction

The International Space Station (*below* and *right*) has been constructed over several years. The first stage was the delivery of the central connecting structure (**1**) in 1998. During the second stage, three astronauts boarded the station (**2**). In the third stage many of the scientific modules were added (**3**). In the year 2000, a full-time crew finally occupied the station for the first time (**4**).

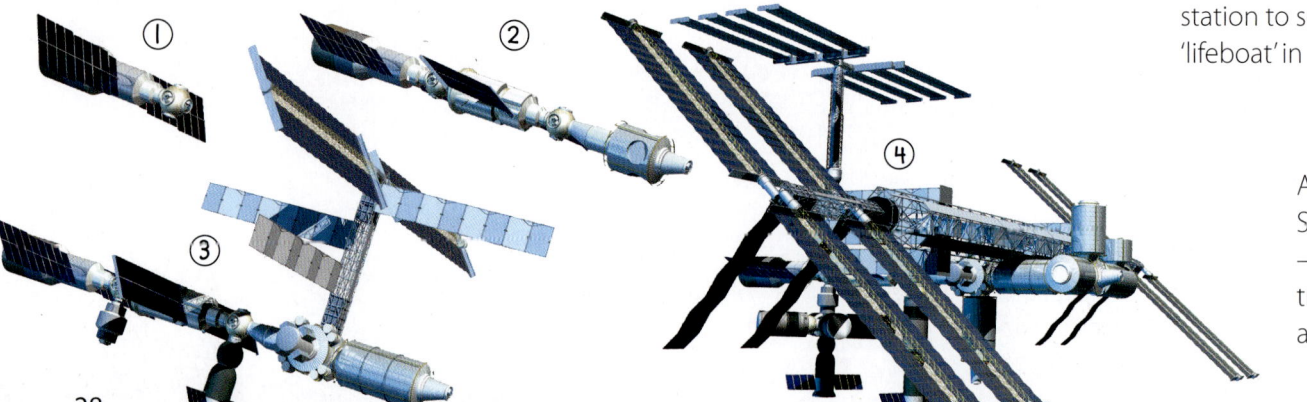

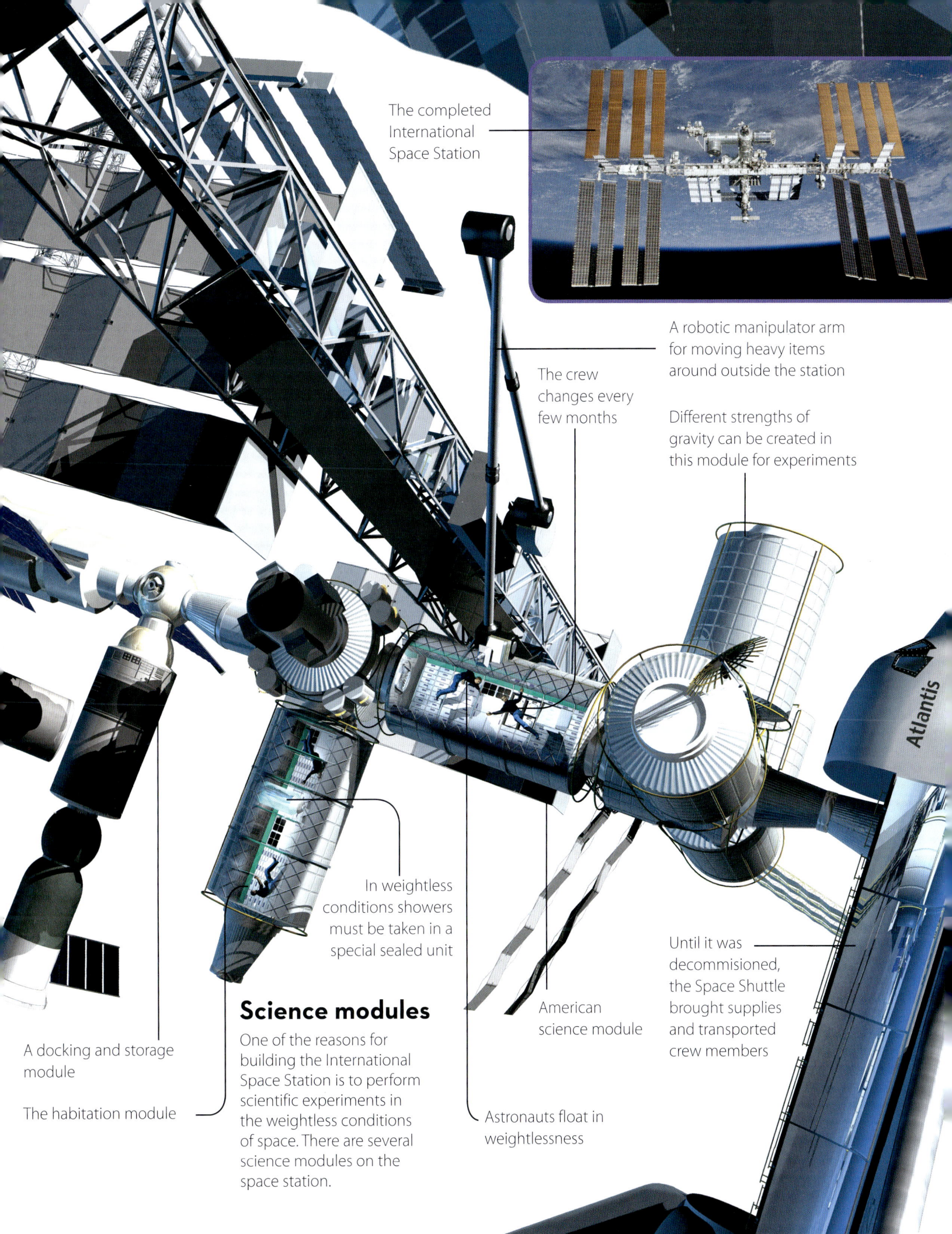

The completed International Space Station

A robotic manipulator arm for moving heavy items around outside the station

The crew changes every few months

Different strengths of gravity can be created in this module for experiments

In weightless conditions showers must be taken in a special sealed unit

Until it was decommissioned, the Space Shuttle brought supplies and transported crew members

American science module

Astronauts float in weightlessness

Science modules

One of the reasons for building the International Space Station is to perform scientific experiments in the weightless conditions of space. There are several science modules on the space station.

A docking and storage module

The habitation module

Viking Lander

The Viking missions were the first to have landers successfully touch down on the surface of Mars. The project was begun in 1968. Because there was a risk of the Viking spacecraft breaking down, two were built. If one didn't work, the other could carry on with the mission. In fact, both space probes worked very well. They landed in the summer of 1976 and worked for many years. Along with the landers, each of the Viking space probes had a section that stayed in orbit. Together, the two Viking orbiters surveyed and mapped nearly all of the planet's surface.

Many scientists think that Mars was once very like Earth. There is evidence that parts of its surface were once covered in water. This means that life may have started on Mars, too. The Viking landers had special equipment on board to test the soil in case it contained tiny living organisms called microbes. But the tests did not find evidence of any form of life.

The Viking landings

The site of Viking 1's touchdown was Chryse Planitia, near to the Martian equator. Viking 2 landed further north in Utopia Planitia. Both areas are flat and desert-like. Heavily cratered areas were avoided in case they damaged the landing spacecraft.

This dish antenna sent information to Earth and received commands

The cameras observed a test pattern to get their colour balance right

Magnets on the test chart were sensitive to magnetic activity on Mars

A machine for measuring earthquakes didn't detect any on Mars

Viking used two cameras to take pictures of the Martian surface

Power generators under protective cover

Fuel tank

Martian soil is red in colour because it is covered in iron oxide, or rust

Flight path

It took the Viking space probes less than a year to reach Mars. Once in the planet's orbit, images of its surface were transmitted to Earth so that scientists could select landing sites. When a site was chosen, the lander was released from the orbiter and a parachute attached to it slowed it down so that it would land gently.

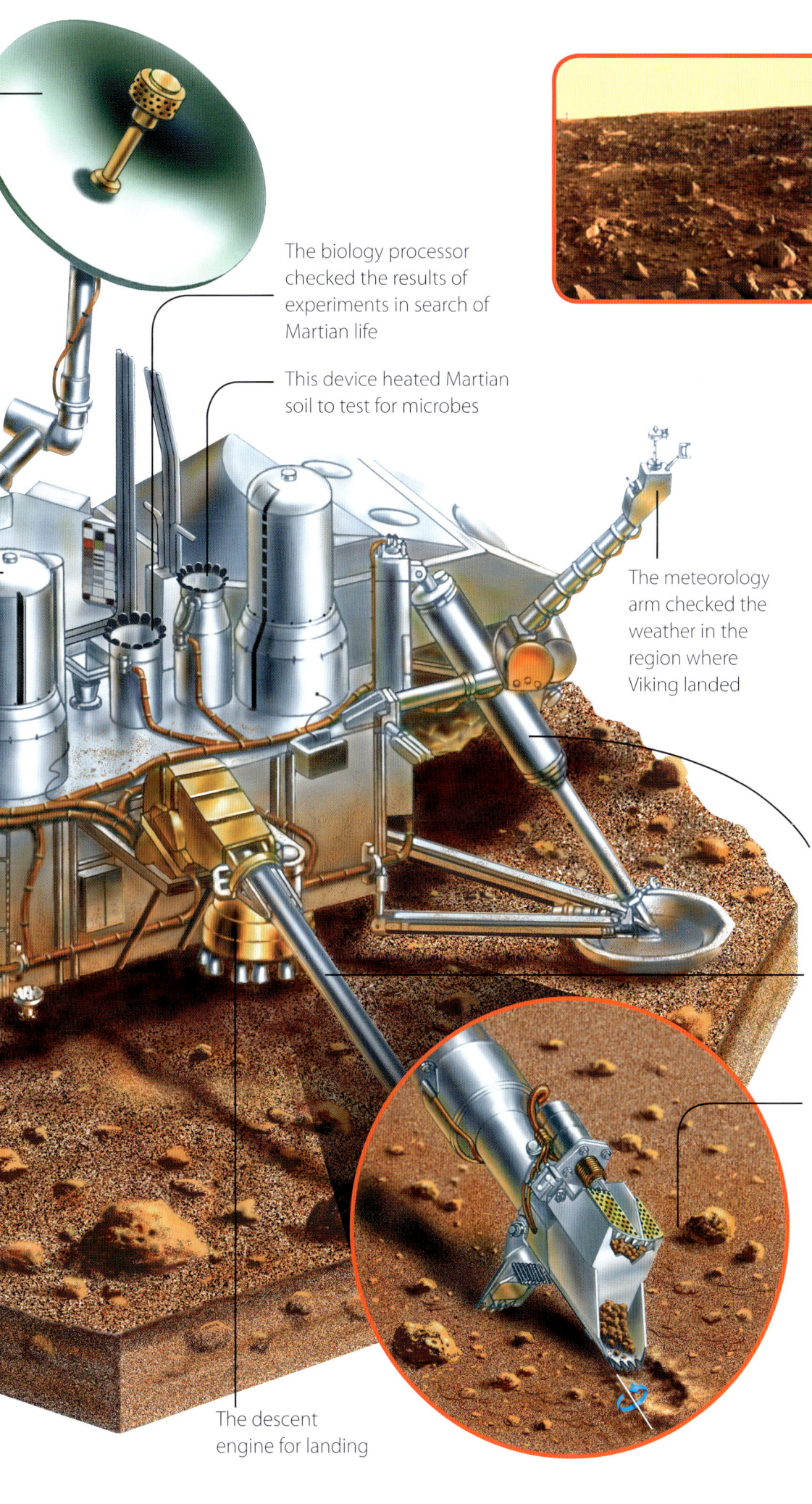

The biology processor checked the results of experiments in search of Martian life

This device heated Martian soil to test for microbes

The meteorology arm checked the weather in the region where Viking landed

The descent engine for landing

Pictures of Mars

Viking 1 began transmitting pictures (like the photo *above*) to Earth just 25 seconds after it touched down on Mars. Because of the long distance from Mars to Earth, the pictures took 19 minutes to arrive by a radio signal. One picture showed a large rock. NASA scientists called it 'Big Joe'. There were fewer big rocks in the region where Viking 2 touched down.

Shock absorbers on the landing legs prevented Viking being damaged during touchdown

The robotic arm on Viking 1 would not work properly in the cold Martian morning

The surface of Mars is covered in soil and rocks

The robotic arm

Viking was designed to test the surface of Mars for signs of life. It did this by scooping soil from the surface and dropping it into the biology processor and heating device. The robotic arm was sent commands from Earth, which it then carried out automatically.

31

Mars Pathfinder

The Mars Pathfinder mission landed on Mars on 4 July 1997. It was the first spacecraft to land on the planet since Viking 1 and 2. There are rock features on Mars that could only have been produced by flowing water. Yet, today, there seems to be hardly any water on the planet. It is hoped that missions like the Mars Pathfinder will help us to find out what happened to it. Pathfinder was a success and returned data for several weeks, even though conditions on Mars were harsh.

Mars Pathfinder was the first mission in an ambitious programme of space probes built to visit Mars. Another, called the Mars Global Surveyor, was sent shortly afterwards to map the planet. Since then, larger rovers Spirit and Opportunity, and the car-sized Curiosity, have each explored even more of Mars's surface. In July 2020, NASA launched Mars 2020, sending another rover similar to Curiosity, called Perseverance, and a small helicopter, Ingenuity, to investigate the surface and look for evidence that there was once life on Mars.

Mars landscape

Mars Pathfinder was designed to land on an ancient flood plain. It is estimated that the flood took place several billion years ago. The surface has remained virtually unchanged since then. The lander came to rest in a small dip. Mars Pathfinder took 16,000 images of Mars. Some (*above*) showed the Sojourner rover at work.

Mars rover

Mars Pathfinder's rover was called Sojourner. It drove across the surface of the planet and went up close to many of the rocks near the Pathfinder to analyse them. Sojourner found volcanic rocks and rocks that had been eroded by wind.

The rover analysed 15 rocks in detail

Solar panels on Mars Pathfinder's petals and on top of Sojourner collected energy

The APXS instrument fired tiny particles at the rocks and measured how the particles rebounded

Sojourner's wheels had spikes to grip the soil

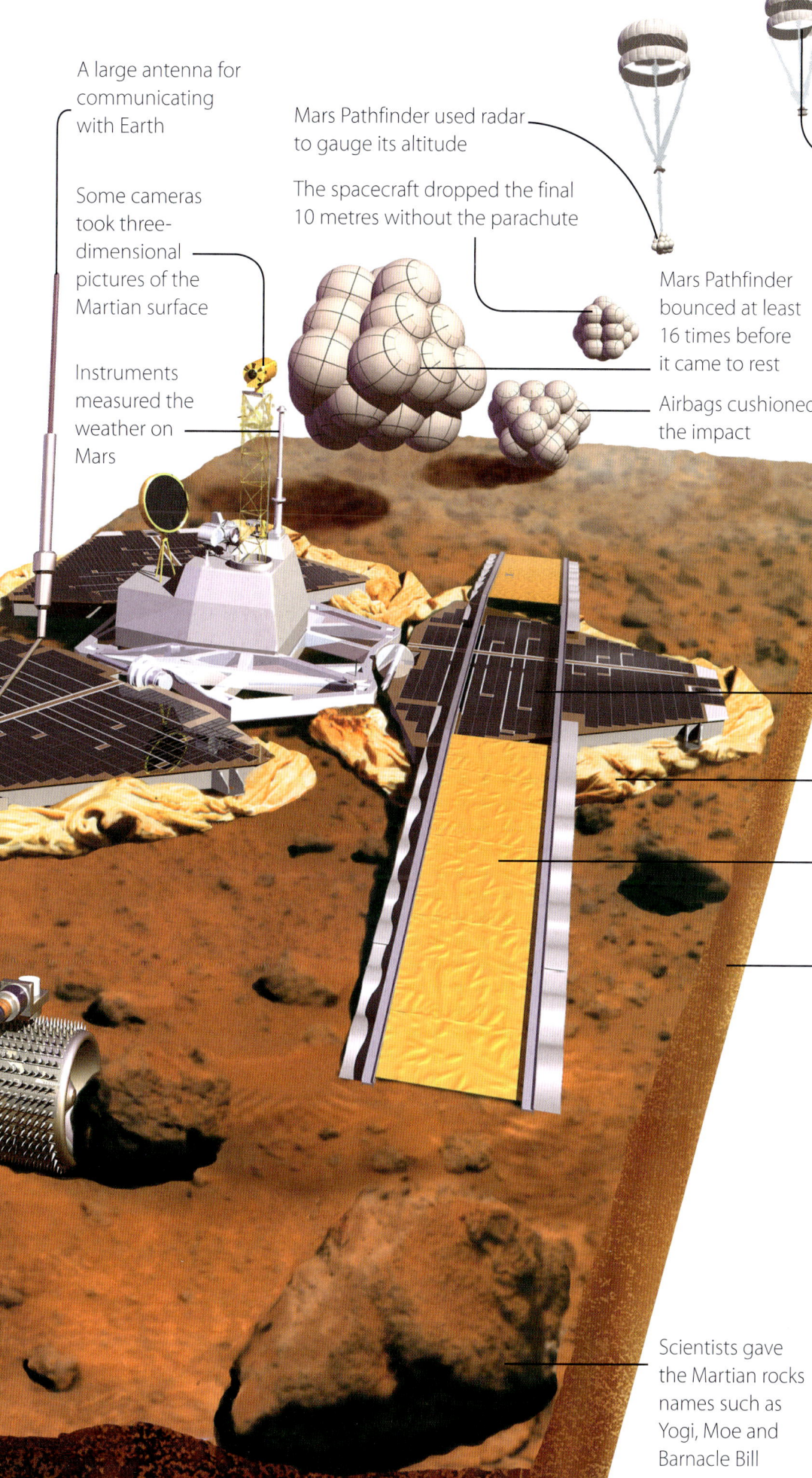

A large antenna for communicating with Earth

Some cameras took three-dimensional pictures of the Martian surface

Instruments measured the weather on Mars

Mars Pathfinder used radar to gauge its altitude

The spacecraft dropped the final 10 metres without the parachute

Mars Pathfinder bounced at least 16 times before it came to rest

Airbags cushioned the impact

Mars Pathfinder entered the atmosphere 125 kilometres above Mars

The parachute opened 10 kilometres above the surface

Sojourner was stored on one of the three petals that opened up after landing

After Mars Pathfinder came to rest, the airbags deflated

A ramp unrolled from the petal, and Sojourner drove onto the Martian surface

Water may be found in a permanent frost layer under the surface of Mars

Scientists gave the Martian rocks names such as Yogi, Moe and Barnacle Bill

Landing on Mars

Instead of using bulky rockets to slow it down for landing, Mars Pathfinder was fitted with large airbags. These inflated as it neared the surface and prevented the lander from being damaged as it struck the rocky surface of Mars.

The Mars lander

Mars Pathfinder was split into two vehicles – a lander and a rover. The lander took readings of the Martian weather conditions, such as temperature and wind speed. It stayed in contact with Earth and relayed messages to the rover. It was renamed the Sagan Memorial Station shortly after it landed in honour of the famous scientist Carl Sagan, who had just died.

Voyager

Two of the most ambitious space missions ever were those of the space probes Voyager 1 and 2. Voyager 2 was launched on 20 August 1977, and Voyager 1 a few weeks later on 5 September 1977. Voyager 1 followed a faster route to Jupiter and overtook Voyager 2 on the way.

In March 1979, Voyager 1 flew by Jupiter and transmitted scientific information and images of the planet to Earth. It continued on, flying by Saturn and its largest moon, Titan, in November 1980. Voyager 2 reached Jupiter in July and Saturn in 1981. Unlike Voyager 1, it did not fly close to Titan. Instead, it continued to Uranus. In January 1986, it transmitted pictures of that pale blue-green planet before continuing its journey onward to Neptune. In August 1989, Voyager 2 reached Neptune – the final flyby of its mission.

It was not until 2015 that the even more distant dawrf planet Pluto was visited by a probe, NASA's New Horizons spacecraft.

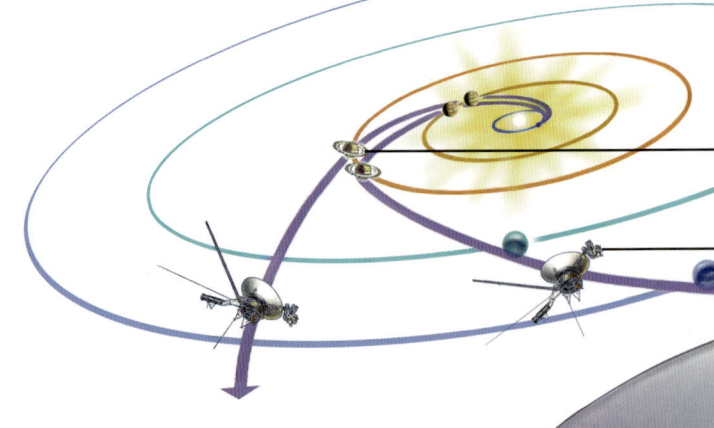

The grand tour

The Voyager space probes followed paths, or trajectories, that made use of gravity-assists. These trajectories were first worked out in 1965 by Gary Flandro, who realised that the four gas giants (*see page 10*) line up once every 175 years. This alignment meant that a probe could visit the gas giants in turn and use each planet's gravity to propel it onwards to the next. He calculated that they would next line up in the 1980s, and so the idea for the Voyager missions was born.

A golden record onboard contains music, sounds and greetings spoken in 55 languages

Voyager 1

On 17 February 1998, Voyager 1 became the most distant object made by humans as it cruised out of the Solar System. It is now over 24 billion kilometres from the Earth.

The magnetometer boom contains detectors that measure magnetic fields in space

The Sun is too faint to be an energy source in the outer Solar System, so radioisotope thermoelectric generators provide Voyager with energy

Fuel from this tank was used by Voyager's thrusters to turn the spacecraft and keep the antenna pointing towards Earth

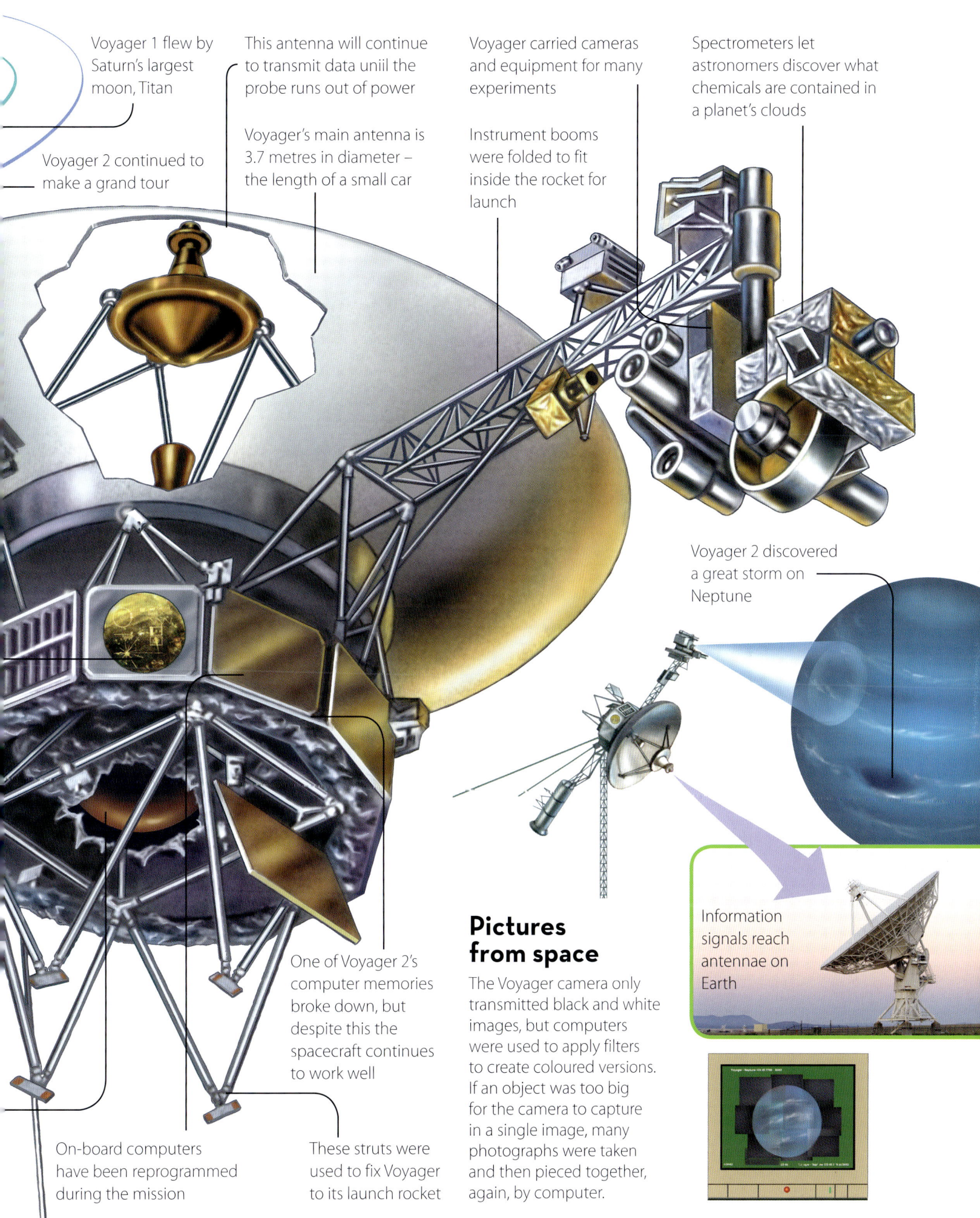

Voyager 1 flew by Saturn's largest moon, Titan

This antenna will continue to transmit data until the probe runs out of power

Voyager carried cameras and equipment for many experiments

Spectrometers let astronomers discover what chemicals are contained in a planet's clouds

Voyager 2 continued to make a grand tour

Voyager's main antenna is 3.7 metres in diameter – the length of a small car

Instrument booms were folded to fit inside the rocket for launch

Voyager 2 discovered a great storm on Neptune

One of Voyager 2's computer memories broke down, but despite this the spacecraft continues to work well

Information signals reach antennae on Earth

On-board computers have been reprogrammed during the mission

These struts were used to fix Voyager to its launch rocket

Pictures from space

The Voyager camera only transmitted black and white images, but computers were used to apply filters to create coloured versions. If an object was too big for the camera to capture in a single image, many photographs were taken and then pieced together, again, by computer.

Studying the Stars

Astronomers use very large telescopes to study the Universe. These telescopes have two mirrors that focus light and are housed in observatories (*right*). Like any piece of equipment, a telescope sometimes needs to be repaired, so everything that is necessary to keep it working is found in the observatory.

Using computer-controlled motors, the telescope operator sitting in the control room can move the telescope. Another astronomer working alongside collects data. A range of cameras and other instruments, known as detectors, can be found in an observatory. Astronomers use them to record their observations by attaching them to the base of the telescope inside a metal cage. Data is fed to the control room and images are then processed and displayed on a computer screen. The images can then be analysed by other astronomers around the world.

Space telescopes

Placing telescopes in outer space avoids interference from Earth's atmosphere and allows astronomers to study the Universe in ways that are not possible from the ground. Space telescopes can 'see' gamma rays, ultraviolet and infrared light, or even X-rays. The James Webb Space Telescope (*below*) was launched in 2021 and is the largest optical telescope in space. It is using infrared light to find some of the oldest and faintest galaxies formed after the Big Bang (*see pages 6–7*).

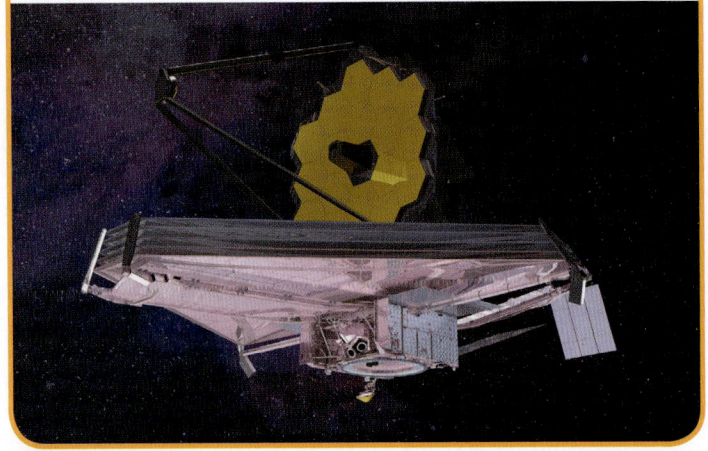

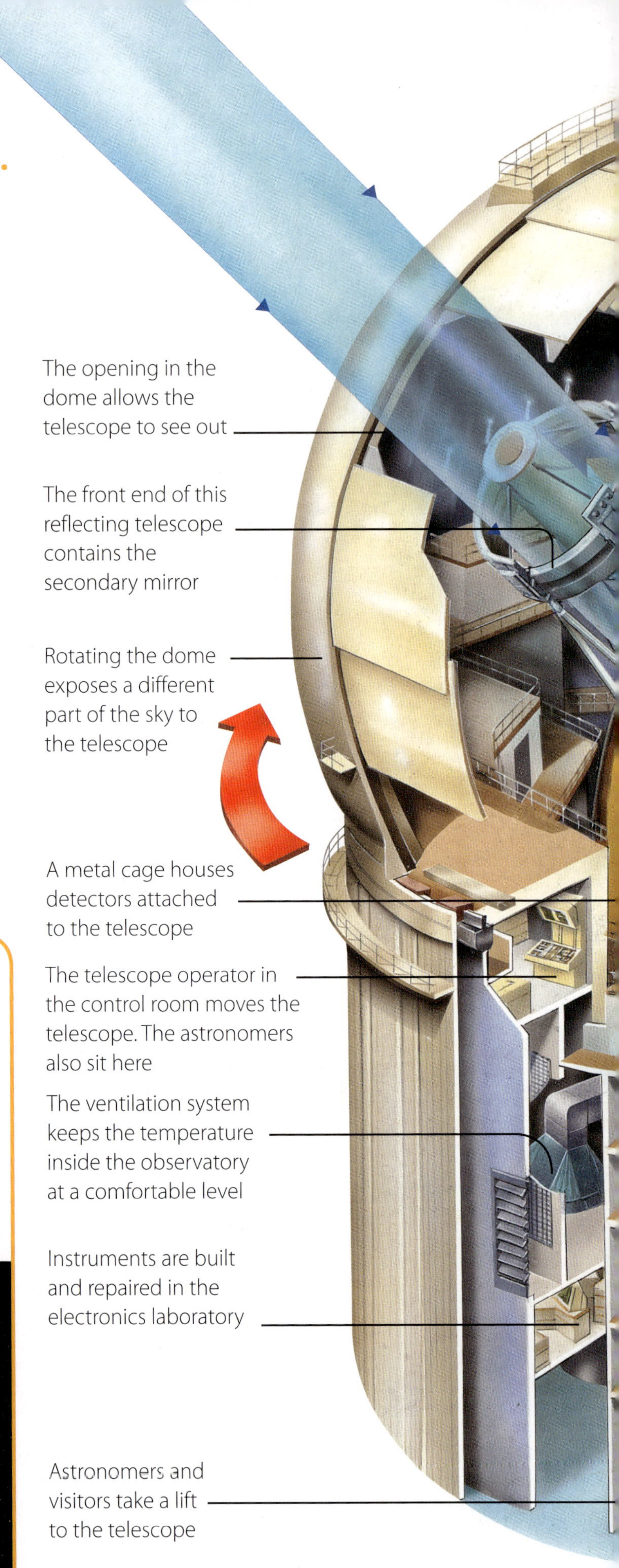

The opening in the dome allows the telescope to see out

The front end of this reflecting telescope contains the secondary mirror

Rotating the dome exposes a different part of the sky to the telescope

A metal cage houses detectors attached to the telescope

The telescope operator in the control room moves the telescope. The astronomers also sit here

The ventilation system keeps the temperature inside the observatory at a comfortable level

Instruments are built and repaired in the electronics laboratory

Astronomers and visitors take a lift to the telescope

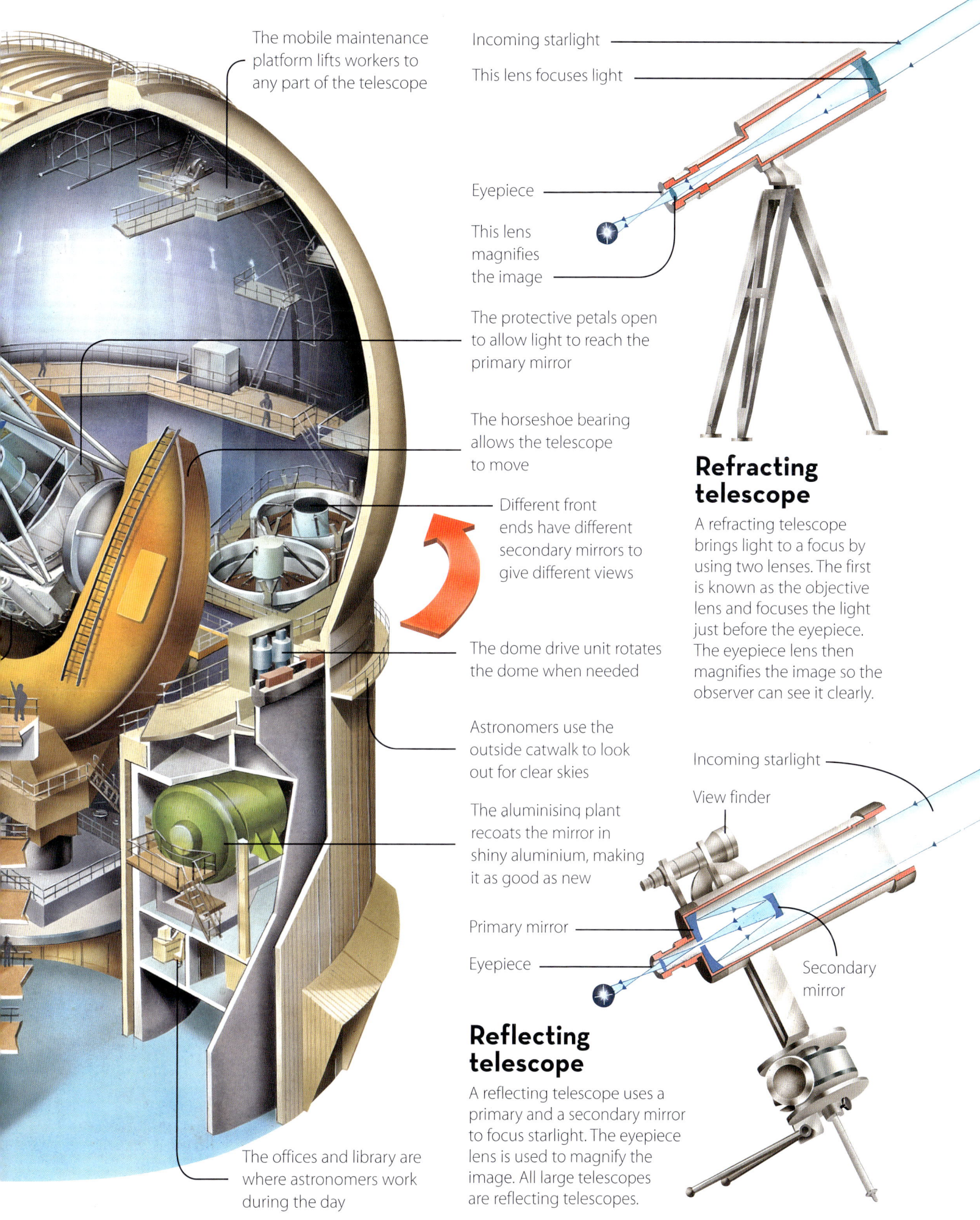

Stars

Stars are enormous energy generators. They are born in collapsing clouds of hydrogen gas. The gas is squeezed so tightly that its temperature rises. When the temperature in the centre of the star reaches 10 million °C, the hydrogen atoms' nuclei collide with such force that they fuse (stick together) and form new nuclei. This nuclear fusion leads to the formation of helium nuclei and the release of energy that makes the star shine.

Stars come in many sizes. The Sun is a little bigger than most other stars, but some stars have a hundred times the mass of the Sun. Stars that contain the most mass do not live as long as stars with little mass. A very high mass star will only live a few million years, while a low mass star, such as the Sun, could last nine billion years or more.

The life of a star

At the first stage of a star's life, the star is the centre of a collapsing gas cloud (1). When the core of a protostar is hot enough, hydrogen begins to fuse and the protostar becomes a star (2). For most of its life a star will generate

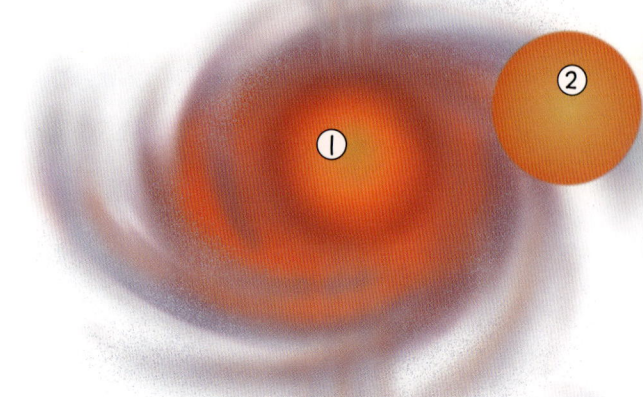

The core of the Sun contains about one tenth of its mass

Energy leaves the Sun's core in light energy particles, called photons

The corona

The outermost gas around the Sun is called the corona. It spreads out very thinly through space and usually cannot be seen because the photosphere of the Sun is so bright. During a solar eclipse, the Moon blocks out the light from the photosphere and the dimmer corona can be seen around the edge.

Eruptive prominences throw superheated gas into space

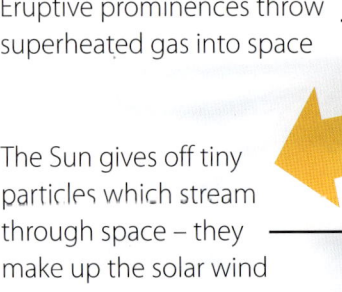

The Sun gives off tiny particles which stream through space – they make up the solar wind

energy and change very little (**3**). As the star grows older it begins to increase in size and generate more energy (**4**). Late in the star's life it begins to pulsate (expand and contract) (**5**). Nuclear fusion takes place in bursts, rather than continuously.

The unstable nuclear fusion in the star lifts its outer layers and throws them off into space. The result is known as a planetary nebula (**6**) because such an object looked like a planet to astronomers in the 1700s.

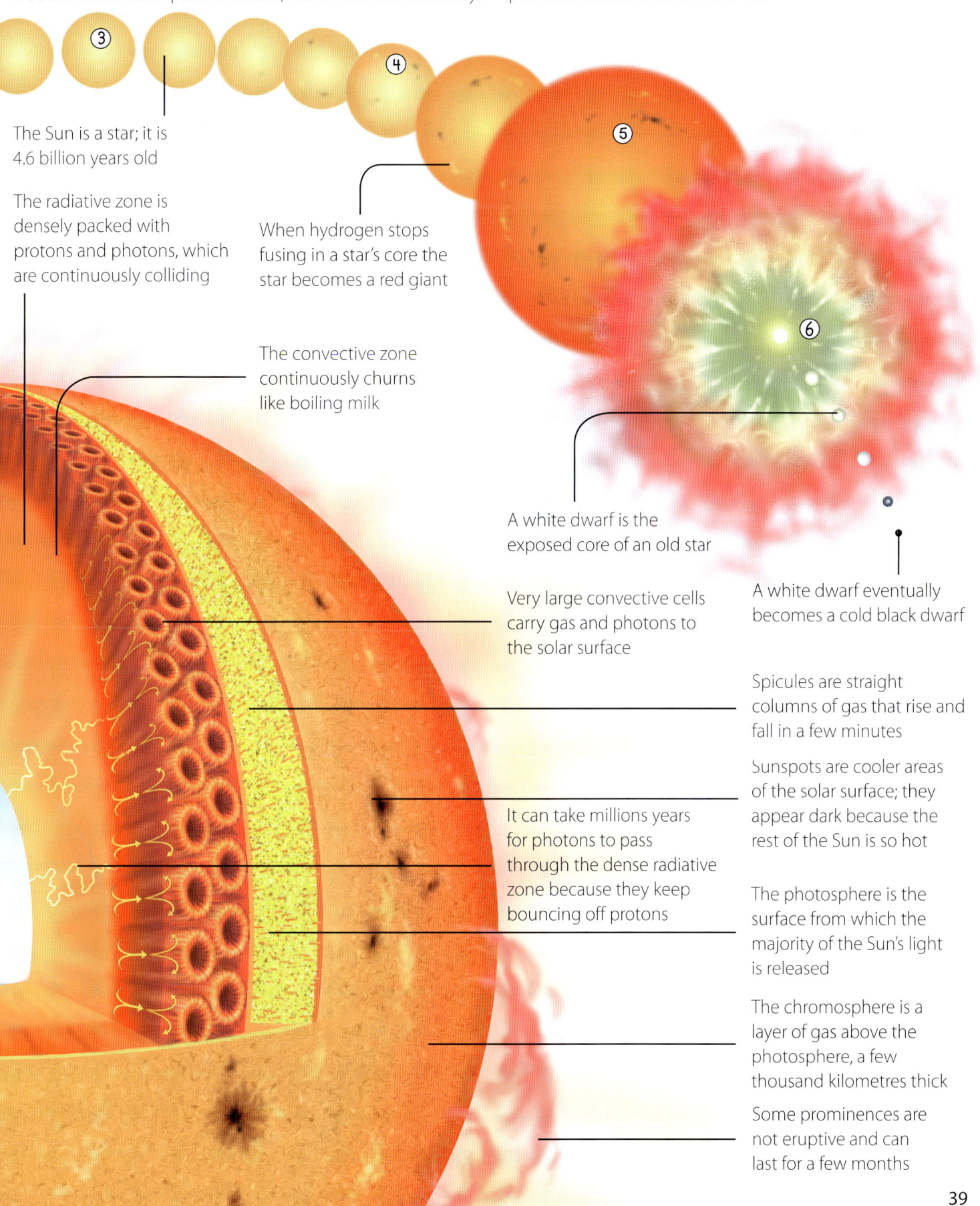

The Sun is a star; it is 4.6 billion years old

The radiative zone is densely packed with protons and photons, which are continuously colliding

When hydrogen stops fusing in a star's core the star becomes a red giant

The convective zone continuously churns like boiling milk

A white dwarf is the exposed core of an old star

Very large convective cells carry gas and photons to the solar surface

A white dwarf eventually becomes a cold black dwarf

Spicules are straight columns of gas that rise and fall in a few minutes

It can take millions years for photons to pass through the dense radiative zone because they keep bouncing off protons

Sunspots are cooler areas of the solar surface; they appear dark because the rest of the Sun is so hot

The photosphere is the surface from which the majority of the Sun's light is released

The chromosphere is a layer of gas above the photosphere, a few thousand kilometres thick

Some prominences are not eruptive and can last for a few months

39

Black Holes

A black hole is one of the most remarkable objects in the Universe. It is an incredibly dense object which possesses so much gravity that nothing can escape from it. Light is the fastest thing in the Universe and yet not even light can escape from a black hole.

In order to escape the gravitational pull of the Earth, a rocket must reach a speed of 11.2 kilometres per second. This is known as the escape velocity. If the Earth were squeezed into a smaller volume, making it more dense, its gravitational pull would be greater and the escape velocity would increase. If the Earth were squeezed to the size of a marble, the escape velocity would go up so much that it would be equal to the speed of light (300,000 kilometres a second). At this point, nothing would escape its gravitational pull and the Earth would become a black hole.

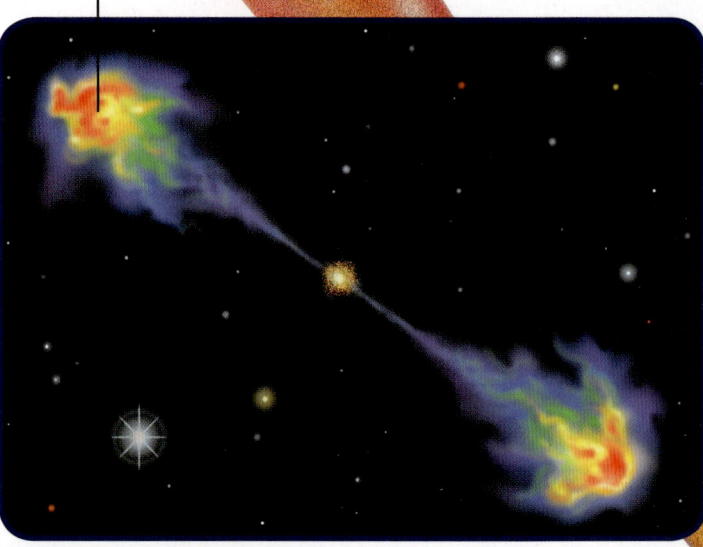

Patches of radio waves at the ends of jets are known as radio lobes

Active galaxies

Some galaxies contain supermassive black holes. These are called active galaxies. Sometimes, jets of particles shoot out from the black hole far into space. The particles collide with each other and produce radio waves which can be picked up by radio telescopes. In the picture above the radio waves have been colour coded by a computer. Only some active galaxies produce radio waves – it is not yet known why.

The torus is a large disc of dust and gas surrounding a supermassive black hole

The torus is often surrounded by clouds of gas that are turning into stars

Stellar black holes

A stellar black hole can be created when a massive star reaches the end of its life. For example, a black hole like IGR J17091 (*right*) can be created when a massive star (**1**) in a binary (double) star system collapses, and gravity pulls in matter around it. The second star (**2**) is pulled apart and swallowed by the black hole. As it orbits the black hole, gas streams from the star onto a disc (**3**) around the black hole before it is consumed. The gas becomes so hot that it gives off X-rays, which can be detected by X-ray telescopes.

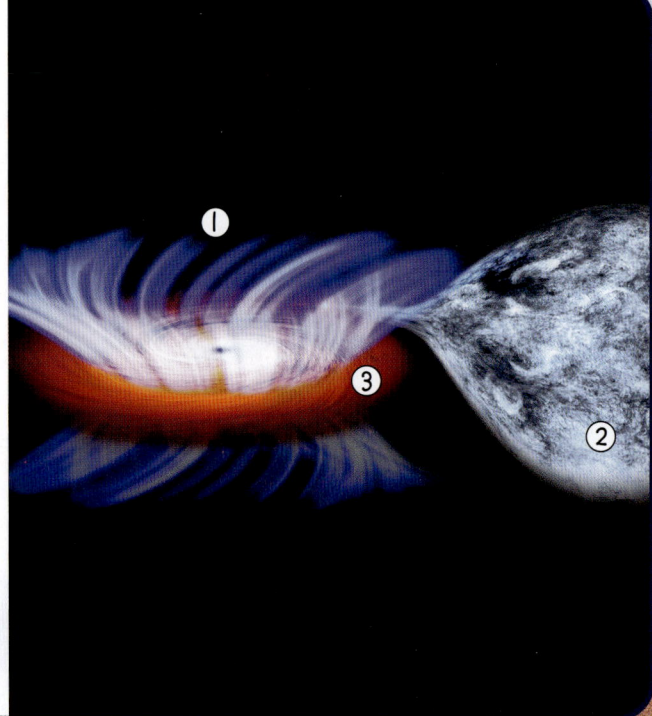

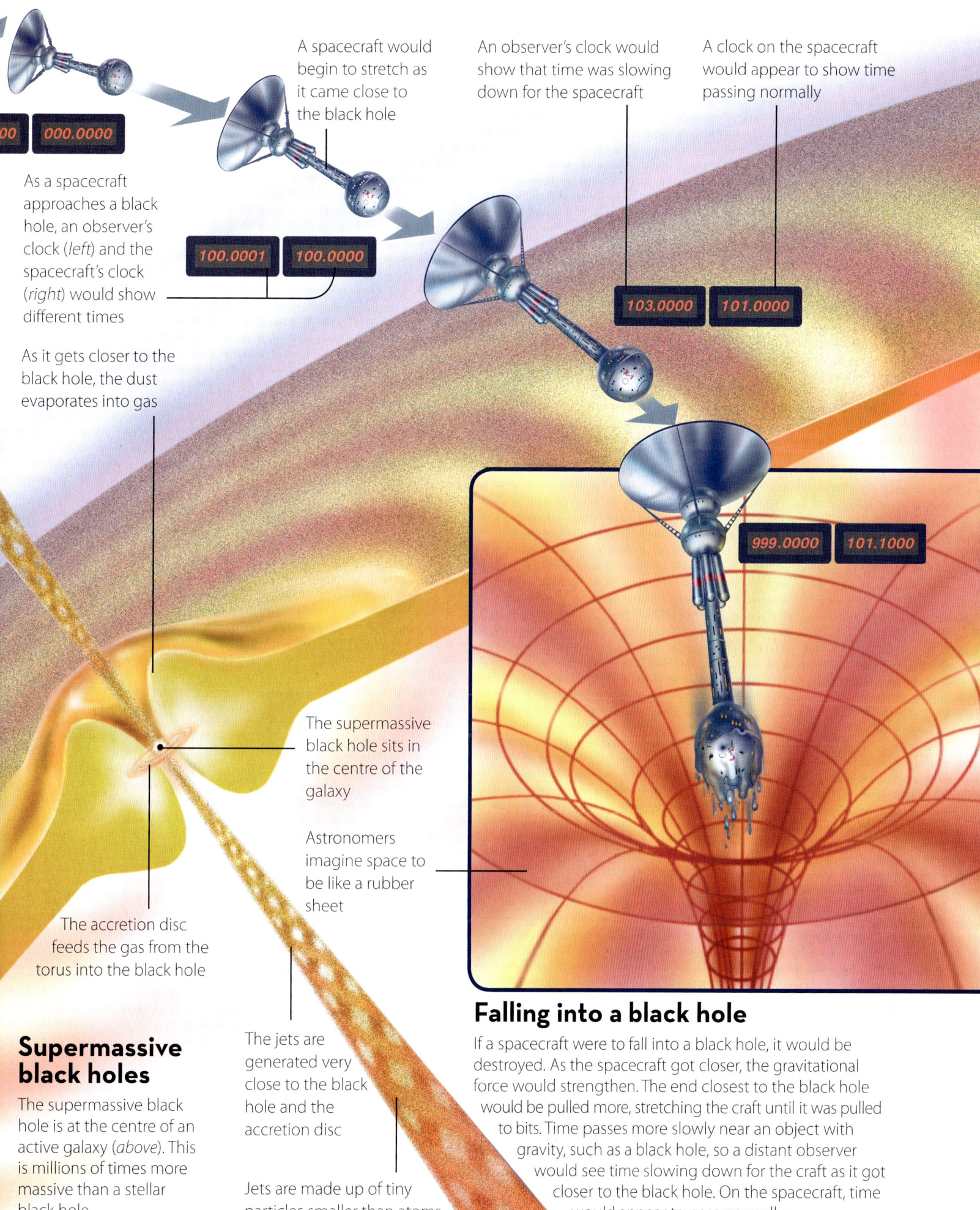

Radio Telescopes

For centuries, telescopes have collected light and focused it into images. However, light is not the only type of radiation released by objects in space. Many also give out radio waves. In order to collect radio waves a special telescope, called a radio telescope, is needed. Radio telescopes are very large dishes which collect radio waves and focus them onto a small detector in the centre of the dish.

The study of radio waves from space has given astronomers new ideas about galaxies. In particular, they have learnt that some active galaxies are powerful emitters of radio waves (*see page 40*). Some astronomers also use radio telescopes to search for messages from space. They are trying to find other life in the Universe, which may communicate using radio waves. No messages have been discovered so far.

The Effelsberg Radio Telescope

The Effelsberg Radio Telescope has a collecting dish with an area of 7,850 square metres. It collects radio waves with this dish and focuses them onto three detectors. The three detectors collect radio waves from three slightly different parts of the sky and this speeds up the process of building an image.

The main dish is like the primary mirror in a reflecting telescope

The radio dish is supported by a strong framework

The waveguides channel the radio waves onto probes

Probes convert the radio waves into electrical signals

Radio images from space

Radio waves picked up by the radio telescope's detectors are combined into a single image. Different radio intensities are colour coded. To obtain higher quality images, several radio telescopes can be used together. Two or more radio telescopes observe the same object at the same time. The signals received by each telescope can then be compared and used to form detailed pictures.

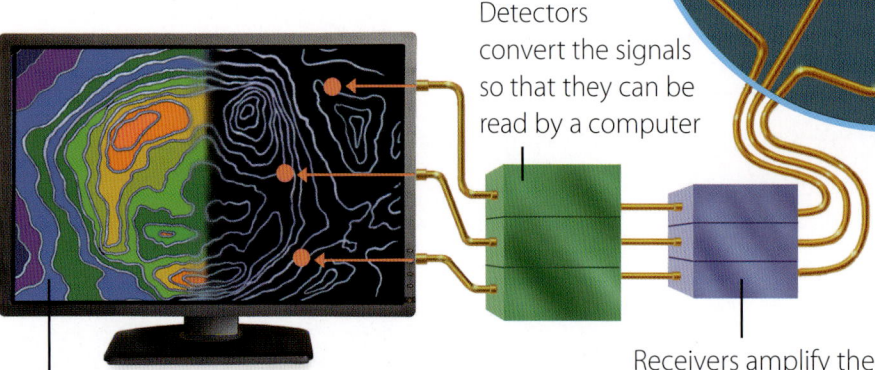

Detectors convert the signals so that they can be read by a computer

A computer displays radio images of an exploded star

Receivers amplify the signals from the probes and pass them to the detectors

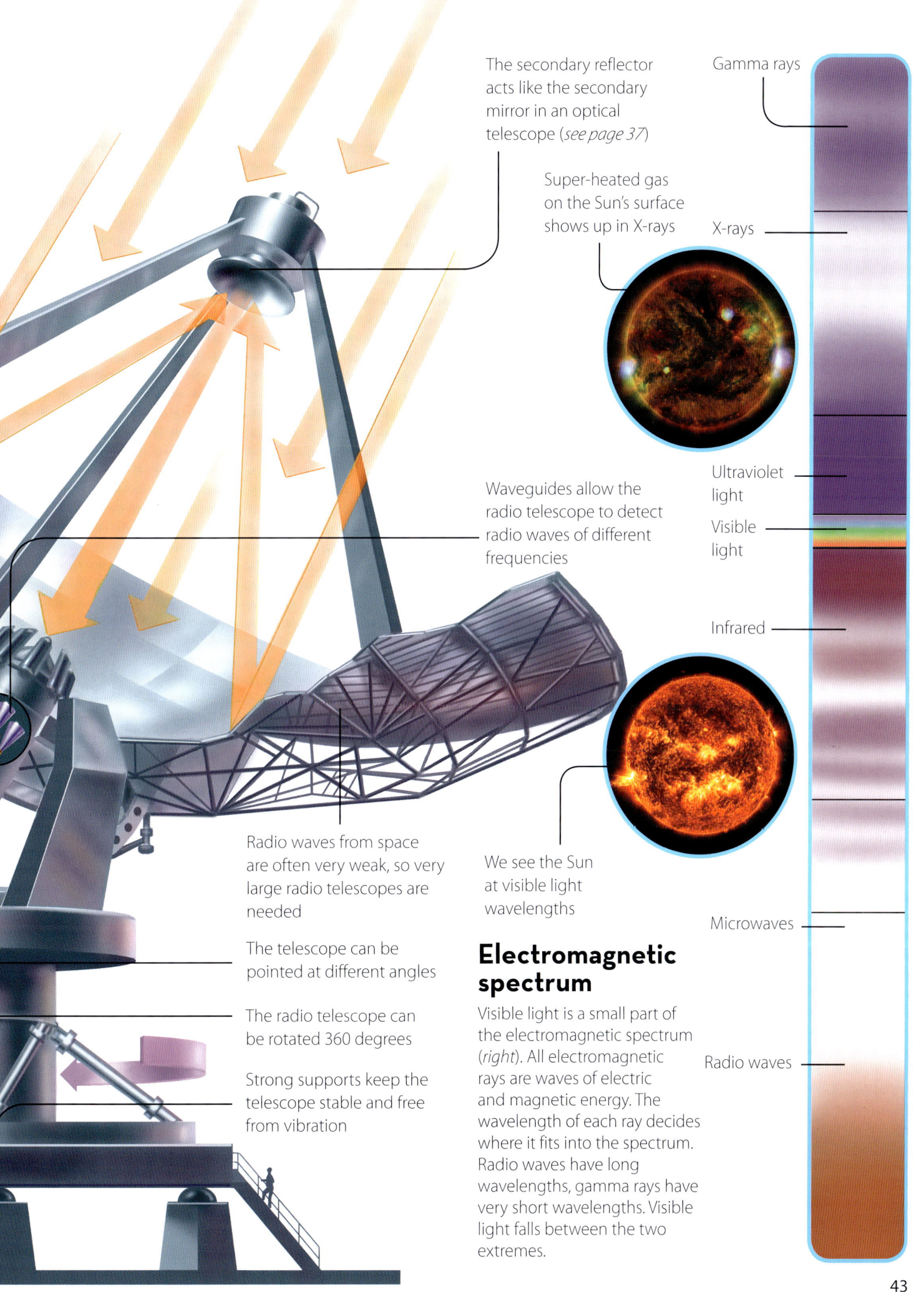

The secondary reflector acts like the secondary mirror in an optical telescope (*see page 37*)

Super-heated gas on the Sun's surface shows up in X-rays

Waveguides allow the radio telescope to detect radio waves of different frequencies

Radio waves from space are often very weak, so very large radio telescopes are needed

We see the Sun at visible light wavelengths

The telescope can be pointed at different angles

The radio telescope can be rotated 360 degrees

Strong supports keep the telescope stable and free from vibration

Gamma rays

X-rays

Ultraviolet light

Visible light

Infrared

Microwaves

Radio waves

Electromagnetic spectrum

Visible light is a small part of the electromagnetic spectrum (*right*). All electromagnetic rays are waves of electric and magnetic energy. The wavelength of each ray decides where it fits into the spectrum. Radio waves have long wavelengths, gamma rays have very short wavelengths. Visible light falls between the two extremes.

Magnetic Fields

A magnetic field is generated every time an electrically charged object moves. Most of the planets in the Solar System are known to generate magnetic fields. The Earth's magnetic field is generated in its fluid, outer core. This is because the heat of the inner core drives the fluid in the outer core up and around in a process called convection. Because this outer core is made of metal, which can be electrically charged, the convection causes a magnetic field to be generated.

The planets Mercury, Venus and Mars generate magnetic fields in similar ways, but compared to the Earth's, their fields are very weak. In the centre of Jupiter and Saturn, hydrogen gas is compressed to behave like a metal and this generates magnetic fields. In Uranus and Neptune, the generating material is thought to be ice.

Auroral display
Tiny particles carrying electrical charges are continuously streaming away from the Sun. Sometimes these get caught in the Earth's magnetic field and are drawn into the atmosphere near the North and South Poles. When these charged particles hit molecules in the atmosphere, they cause them to glow. This is known as an auroral display.

Magnetic poles
All of the magnetic fields behave as if a gigantic bar magnet were buried in the centre of the planet. Invisible lines of magnetic force come out through the magnetic north pole of the planet and back in through the magnetic south pole. (The magnetic poles are at opposite ends to the geographic poles.)

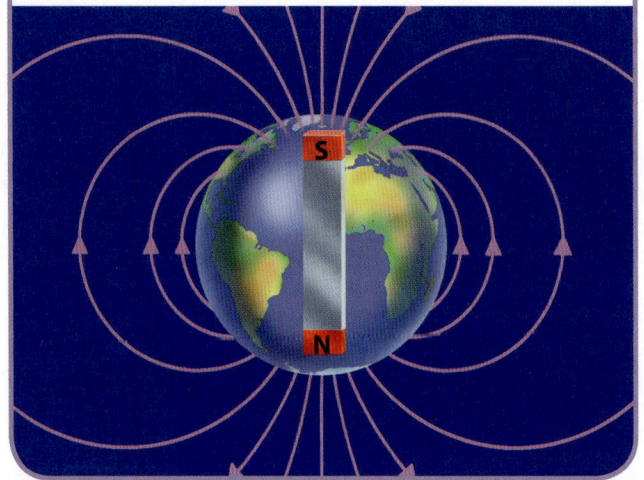

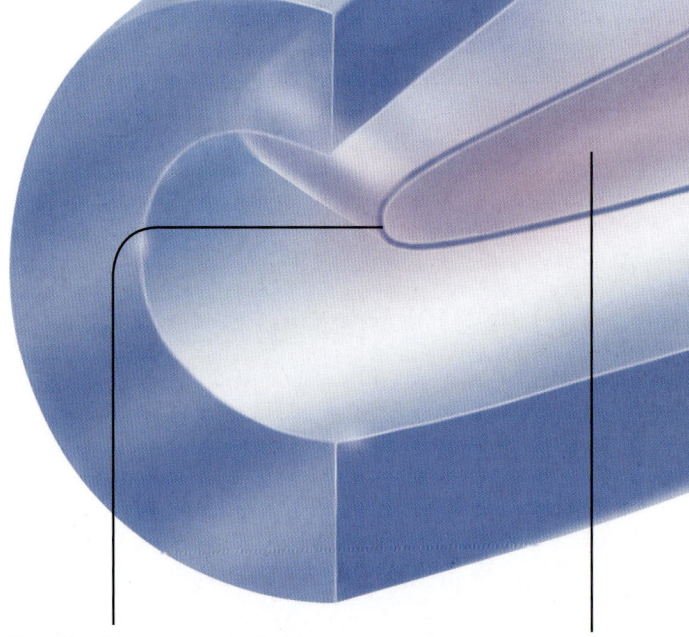

The magnetosphere protects the Earth from the harmful charged particles of the solar wind

Most particles from the Sun stream past the Earth

The Earth's magnetic field stretches away from the Sun for millions of kilometres

Some particles are caught and trapped in the plasma sheet

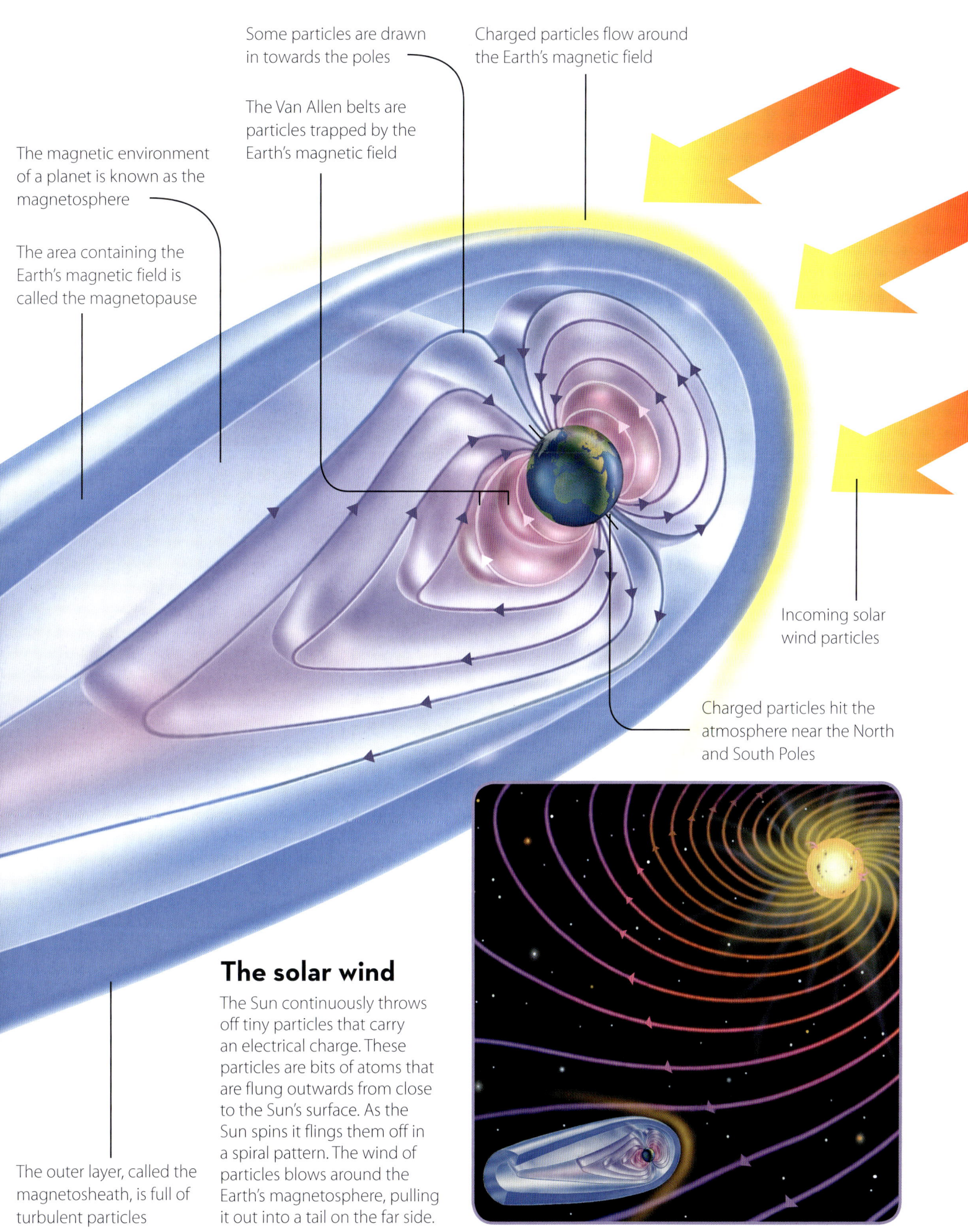

Index

A
Andromeda 8
Apollo missions 16, 20–23
Ariane rocket 17
Armstrong, Neil 20
asteroid belt 10, 11
astronauts 18, 20, 22–24, 26–29
atmosphere 15
attitude jets 26
auroral display 44

B
Big Bang 6–7
black holes 40–41

C
Canaveral, Cape 24
celestial sphere 15
Charon 12
comets 14
command and service module 18
control box, spacesuit 27
corona 38

E
early missions 18–19
Earth 10, 11, 14–15
  magnetic field 44–45
  orbit 9, 14
Effelsberg Radio Telescope 42–43
ejection, astronaut 18–19
electromagnetic spectrum 43
elliptical orbit 9
emergency procedure 19
escape velocity 40
Europa 12
expanding Universe 9

F
flight path 17
fuel tank 16, 17, 24

G
Gagarin, Yuri 18
galaxies 6–7, 8–9, 36
  active 40
  barred-spiral 8
  elliptical 8
  Milky Way 7, 8–9, 10
  spiral 8
Goddard, Robert 16

gravity 10

H
habitation module 28
Hubble, Edwin 9
Humason, Milton 9

I
instrument module 18
International Space Station 26, 28–29
Io 12

J
James Webb Space Telescope 36
Jupiter 10–11, 12–13, 34, 44

L
landing
  on Earth 18–19, 21, 25
  on Mars 31–32
  module 20–21
  on Moon 20–21, 22, 30
light year 8
Lunar Prospector 22
lunar rock 23
lunar roving vehicle 22–23

M
magnetic fields 44–45
magnetic poles 44
manned moon missions 20
mantle (Earth's) 14
Mars 10, 12, 13, 44
  Global Surveyor 32
  landing on 31–33
  Pathfinder 32–33
  pictures of 31
  rover 32–33
  Viking lander 30–31
matter 6, 12
Mercury 10, 13, 44
Milky Way 7, 8–9, 10
Mir 28
Moon (of Earth) 12
  missions to 16, 20–23
  orbit 9
  phases 11
moons of planets 12, 34, 35

N
Neptune 10, 11, 12, 34, 44

Newton, Sir Isaac 16

O
orbits 8, 9
  Earth 9, 14
  Moon 9
  planets 10
  rockets and spacecraft 19, 20, 21

P
Pathfinder 32–33
payload 16
planets 8, 9, 12–13
  magnetic fields 44–45
  orbits 10
  see also Earth
Pluto 10, 11, 12
Portable Life Support System (PLSS) 22

Q
quarks 6

R
radio telescopes 42–43
redshift 9
rings 10, 12
robotic arm 31
rocket fuel 16, 17
rockets and spacecraft 16–17
  Apollo 16, 20–23
  in black hole 41
  flight profile 18
  orbits 19, 20, 21
  Space Shuttle 16, 24–25, 29
  space stations 28–29
  Vostok 18–19
  Voyager 34–35
rocks 23, 31, 33
rotation, Earth 15

S
Salyut 28
satellites 16, 24–25
Saturn 10, 11, 12, 13, 35, 44
Saturn V (rocket) 16
science modules 29
seasons 14
Skylab 28
Sojourner 32–33
Solar System 7, 9, 10–11
solar wind 45
Soyuz 16, 28

space probes 22, 34–35
Space Shuttle 16, 24–25, 29
space stations 28–29
space telescopes 36
space walking 26–27
spacecraft *see* rockets
spacesuit 26–27
stars 15, 36–37, 38–39
Sun 8, 10, 11, 38–39
sunspots 39
superclusters 8
surveyor probes 22, 23

T
telescopes 36–37, 42–43
Tereshkova, Valentina 18
Titan 12, 34, 35

U
Universe 8–9
Uranus 10, 12, 44

V
Venus 10, 13, 44
Viking landers 30–31
Vostok 18–19
Voyager 34–35